How To Love Your Inner Human In A World Of Anxiety

Self Help Solutions To Not Feeling Good Enough

By

JOHN CRAWFORD

ISBN-10: 1794226486
ISBN-13: 978-1794226487

Copyright © 2019 by John Crawford

All rights reserved.

First Published: February 2019

www.youcanfixyouranxiety.com

No part of this book may be reproduced in any form or by any electronic or mechanical means including information storage and retrieval systems, without permission in writing from the author. Short quotes are permissible providing that credit is given to this author in the quoting work.

Every effort has been made in the writing of this book to give credit where it is due, including short quotes, and there is no intention to infringe upon any copyrights. If you believe that there is any part of this work which infringes your intellectual property in any way please let me know and I will gladly remove it immediately.

Please visit: http://www.youcanfixyouranxiety.com for updates, offers, news, enquiries, and events.

Disclaimer

I am a fully-qualified experienced hypno/psychotherapist. I am not a medically trained Doctor or Psychiatrist. I have taken every care to ensure that the information presented in this book is both ethical and responsible, and the information and techniques within this have been safely used with my clients during my career.

However, if you have been diagnosed with, or believe you may be suffering from any form of psychiatric condition, you should seek professional help, and you should not use this book without the consent and blessing of your qualified formal medical healthcare provider. To all readers, please ensure that you read, understand, and agree to the following disclaimer before proceeding:-

This book is provided on an "as is" basis. I cannot assess nor guarantee that this book is suitable for your needs, or for use by you. You use this book at your own risk. The information offered in this book is offered as complementary therapeutic information. Information and content offered throughout this book are not offered as medical treatment, or diagnosis of a medical condition, and no such suggestion may be implied by you or me. If you are suffering from any medical condition or believe that you may need medical or psychiatric treatment, you are advised to see your Doctor or formal healthcare provider. By your use of this book, no medical, advisory, therapeutic, or professional relationship is implied or established between you and myself. Any information provided in this book is for information purposes only and does not replace or amend your Doctor's advice. Any action you may take arising from your use of this book, or any of the exercises contained within, including the use of relaxation recording/s, is undertaken entirely at your own risk and discretion. If any of the exercises contained within this book make you feel uncomfortable or distressed in any way, you agree to discontinue using them immediately. Use of this book does not guarantee a cure of any mental, emotional, or medical condition, and no such suggestion may be implied. This book and the information contained within it have not been audited by any official bodies, either professional, regulatory, or governmental.

JOIN ME IN MY READERS GROUP

As a valued reader, I'd like to invite you to join me by becoming a member of my free reader's group and download my third book "Dear Anxiety: This Is My Life" **plus** two professionally recorded relaxation recordings, delivering authentic hypnosis experiences for beating stress – all **absolutely free of charge.** No strings. Just sign up with your email address and I'll add you to the group. You can unsubscribe at any time.

When John's frantic search for spiritual accomplishment delivered way more than he expected, things suddenly got extremely weird! A reality-shattering event propelled John, an ordinary twenty two year old Londoner, into a terrifying world where the very fabric of reality itself could not be trusted. This sounds like fiction.

It is not.

Get John's FREE full ebook today and find out what it took to get home...

Download your free copy instantly below!

Here's the link:-

http://www.youcanfixyouranxiety.com/amazon-book-free-gift

Contents

- Disclaimer 3
- Join Me In My Readers Group 4
- Introduction 8
- Chapter One – Original Innocence 15
- Chapter Two – Monkeys And Angels 25
- Chapter Three – Let's Talk About Parents 30
- Chapter Four – Self-Esteem Versus Self-Worth 34
- Chapter Five – A Surprising Revelation 38
- Chapter Six – Your Heart Is In The Right Place 43
- Chapter Seven – Morality & Hypocrisy 48
- Chapter Eight - Understanding Hatred 56
- Chapter Nine - Failure And Success 58
- Chapter Ten – Judgement 61
- Chapter Eleven - A Rising Tide Lifts All Boats 69
- Chapter Twelve – We Don't Know Enough 73
- Chapter Thirteen – Culture 90
- Chapter Fourteen - Body Shame 96
- Chapter Fifteen – Other People 108
- Chapter Sixteen – Acceptance 117
- Chapter Seventeen - Getting To The Roots Of Your Feelings 133
- Chapter Eighteen – Self Forgiveness 147

Chapter Nineteen - Recovering Your Personal Power	158
Chapter Twenty – Who's Got Your Back?	169
Chapter Twenty One – Dealing With Bullies	174
Chapter Twenty Two -Trusting Yourself	181
Chapter Twenty Three – Owning Your Voice	191
Chapter Twenty Four – Anxiety And Your Mind	201
Chapter Twenty Five - You've Got This!	206
One Last Thing	209
Stay Connected	209
Other Works By This Author	210
Free Book Offer	213
About John Crawford	214
Full Copyright Notice	216

"I was alone for such a long time. Why did you never speak to me?"

"I didn't know how to."

Introduction

It's not very fashionable to talk about loving yourself. For some, the idea conjures up images of people who think way too much of themselves. Others may regard the concept as saccharin-sweet indulgent nonsense dreamt up by out of touch utopians to sell a non-existent nirvana to the gullible and misguided. In some ways the naysayers may be right. It really depends on your definition of self-love.

If self-love is defined as being all starry-eyed about how wonderful you are and what a blessing each moment of life is, then it's not surprising that many people have no time for the idea. Real life is demanding, most of us are just plain "ordinary", and existence is not all love and light is it? Some of us may be feeling increasingly irrelevant amidst the march of social media, technological advancement, and information overload. This; however, is precisely **why** we need to be loving towards ourselves. The last thing any of us need is to be doing battle with ourselves when we've got so much else on our plates.

This book isn't a handbook for the vain. Quite the opposite in fact. It's for people who need a helping hand in remembering and reclaiming their core sense of value. You exist. That's valuable. **You** are valuable. I'm going to give you a book's worth of perspectives and tools here, to know right down to the core of your being, that wherever you are right now...you **are** good enough!

I don't mind admitting to you that I am secretly a little envious of people who manage to live super-healthy, low-impact lifestyles. In my dreams, I have a six-pack (abs, not beer), I'm 100% environmentally friendly, and I never put a foot wrong. I wake up each morning with a sense of supreme joy and satisfaction that I am a great and virtuous one; a champion of the Earth. Nobody can accuse me of hypocrisy or culpability. My mind and body are in perfect balance in every joyful minute of each beautiful day.

It's never going to happen. I'm a Lazy Libran with a Taurus moon. That's a double whammy. Both signs are lazy, pleasure loving bliss-bunnies. That's code for being generally undisciplined. No, I am not Tony Robbins, I do not work out every day, I have a twelve pack and it's not muscle, and my message is not that you need to work harder, or be better, to feel okay about yourself.

If star-signs aren't your thing, then my next best excuse for my lack of perfection is that I'm an ex-depression sufferer. I find life difficult enough without having to worry whether I have the right brand of yogurt, or indeed whether said yogurt will expand my waistline by a millimetre. Yes, I would love to be perfect, and I have tried. What I discovered during my many attempts to obtain this elusive prize though is that the price tag is so far past unaffordable that I am usually bankrupt by Sunday. I'm old enough now to know that it's unlikely to happen. I'm just not vain enough. But you know what? I like myself, and most of the time I really enjoy life. I wouldn't trade that for a six pack in a million years.

And here's the shocker. I've been a successful therapist for the last fifteen years. To be clear, that means that I've been helping people to overcome the worst habits known to Humanity, recover from every imaginable psychological ailment, and generally be a good dispenser of wise and compassionate counsel. I am supposed to be a shining example of perfect poise.

One night, many years ago, I tumbled out of a nightclub at three in the morning with a drink in one hand and a cigarette in the other, swaying poetically, and looked up to see one of my therapeutic clients (or were there two of her?) standing a few feet away, observing me with wry amusement. I waved tentatively (with my smoking hand), attempted a smile, and was then immediately swallowed up by a fiery hole in the ground. Not one of my finest moments. I have a private life too.

I don't always act in a loving way towards myself either. Sometimes I get it badly wrong, usually when my stress (or excitement) levels are high. I maintain balance for about eighty five percent of the time. Of the remaining fifteen percent, about twelve percent includes being close to on-track but wavering, and the remaining three percent accounts for completely losing the plot. This might include a day of fabulous overeating (summer barbecues, festivals, parties & Xmas...hmmm...num num!), a stupendous hangover (the same), or doing (or not doing) something that I knew would make me feel anxious or low and doing it anyway, because you know...we never learn, do we?

Self-love is down by ninety percent in those three percent days, and quite rightly too. That's a conscience speaking, and we need that to stay alive and healthy. It is necessary that self-love is somewhat conditional. If it were completely unconditional, I'd wager that we'd all be having a drug-fuelled orgy with chocolate cake for dessert right now, and every day thereafter, and be dead within ten years. Some restraint is necessary.

What this book is really about then, is how to love yourself fully **within the limits of a real life**. If you are Mr or Mrs athletic vegan marathon runner, I sincerely doff my cap to you. Kudos! But, most of us aren't, and more importantly never will be, no matter how hard we try. I have driven myself to complete exhaustion in the past in an effort to sculpt my dream body and achieve maximum health and fitness. I've drunk the green sludge. I never got the body I dreamed of but I did get depressed, it did really hurt, and the process itself required nothing less than a complete moment by moment obsession with the goal. For me that felt like mental illness right there, and to be honest, I didn't personally feel any greater sense of well-being. I just felt more tired and hassled and my limbs ached constantly. Some do succeed but it's unsustainable for many people in the long run. You know, even Mr Universe himself has been out of shape a few times.

There is a fine line between self-love and self-abuse, and this works on both sides of the virtue line. Excessive exercise is not self-love but neither is being inactive. Eating right is loving yourself but denying yourself an occasional indulgence is not. It's not just our bodies that require maintenance either. We also have to think about our mental and emotional health too.

If being kind to myself means **never** speaking to myself harshly or feeling pangs of regret, guilt, or shame, then I am likely to live without discipline, and most probably be a menace to myself and the people around me too. This will lead to a lack of competency and achievement, along with various other consequences, and I will suffer as a result. If being kind to myself requires horse-whipping myself into relentless action in every minute of every day with nothing less than perfect outcomes, then I may achieve much but end up thoroughly exhausted, and too depressed to enjoy my achievements. It's admirable to be all that we can be but a failure to recognise our limitations in that process will lead to inevitable burnout. It's tricky isn't it?

I was lucky. I went through a severe and prolonged crisis of anxiety and depression in my twenties which resulted in me arriving at a place of deep hatred towards myself, and life itself. Lucky? How is that lucky? Well, it was an endless living nightmare at the time but it's been over for a long time now so I have the luxury of reaping the benefits of experience. The misery went on for many years and I was genuinely baffled as to why I couldn't recover. I tried just about every therapy going and repeatedly failed to recover my well-being. Consciously, my position at that time was that I was a nice guy who had made a few mistakes but life was now punishing me mercilessly with relentless anxiety and depression for the mistakes I'd made. I saw "life" as the problem, not me.

Eventually, after many wrong turns, I found my way to a couple of therapists who quickly revealed to me that I had in fact been punishing myself. They didn't tell me that this was the case. They skilfully directed me to reveal it to myself. I was rather stunned because consciously I thought that I fundamentally liked who I was. I just didn't like my illness.

Evidently though, **unconsciously** there was a raging, murderous self-hatred taking place, and I discovered that this hatred was so deep that he (my unconscious self) actually wanted me dead. I finally understood one of the reasons that I had felt so awful that I wanted to die. In the second half of the book we'll be exploring these unconscious agendas, and I'll teach you how to identify them, and set them straight. Self-love and emotional protection is going to be difficult, if not impossible, without this knowledge.

I became aware at quite a young age then, that loving oneself is not a luxury, it is a necessity. I count this knowledge a stroke of luck because once I understood it, I placed self-love right at the top of my list of priorities, which has led to a good life. On the face of it, one might conclude that this means that I've led a selfish life. On the contrary, once I started being loving towards myself, my energy and well-being improved exponentially, and I naturally did what people do when they've got spare energy – I served the community.

Self-love is not an act of selfishness. It is a strategy for ensuring that you're well enough to be the best person you can be and have something left to share with others too.

Since I learned this important life lesson, everything I've done since has been shaped and guided by one simple question as a priority:-

Am I being kind to myself?

Living with this question at the front and centre of my being has proven to be highly effective. As a result, I generally tend to make good decisions which lead to fruitful outcomes. These aren't always the easy choices. In fact, being kind to myself often involves choosing a course of action which is unappealing but I've learned that if I don't come through for myself, nobody else will. Here's where the emotional protection part comes in. I want to people please. I like to be liked. I want to help. The pull to say yes when I really need to say no is strong. It's only by placing self-love at the pinnacle of my decision-making process that I can set appropriate limits which ensure my continued well-being. I need to be able to tolerate the guilt which inevitably follows from saying no. Doing so is sometimes an act of self-love. The world asks a lot of each of us. If we can't say no sometimes, we're in hot water.

Life is still challenging at times, but nowadays I have a good friend by my side, and we do what needs to be done, in solidarity, usually with a Dunkirk spirit. That's me and my inner-human. On other occasions, we totally misbehave, have a blast, and pay the price together. The important thing though, is that when the proverbial hits the cooler, I'm there for him and he's there for me. As far as is possible, all actions are undertaken by mutual agreement.

We have some age-old agreements which I count as sacred. I've kept my sincere promises to him faithfully for my entire adult life, and as a result, he trusts me. Sometimes, I still get the small stuff wrong and he gives me hell but we don't fall out. I usually accept a deserved slap gracefully because I know I crossed the line, and I start apologising quickly. Self-love isn't gushing sentimentality. It is a solid, honest, flexible and dependable friendship, that you build with yourself.

Self-love is being able to answer the question "Who's got your back?" with the words "I do", and then having enough flexibility built in to the relationship that you don't beat yourself to a pulp when you screw up. Screwing up is inevitable. Nobody gets everything right all the time.

I've been a therapist for the best part of the last fifteen years of my life now, and this has given me a rather profound insight into the nature of people's relationships with themselves. Of course, I tend to receive a somewhat biased view since people arrive at my door in a state of disharmony but nonetheless, it would seem that self-love doesn't rank very highly in most peoples' priorities. For many it's an entirely new concept.

Not only is self-love misunderstood but it is also hugely undervalued. Being at war with oneself is all too often a central reason that somebody has become depressed or anxious. Feeling like we have to apologise for breathing is a waste of a good life. Loving ourselves may not solve these difficulties alone but it remains a vital and regularly overlooked component of well-being. In addition to being central to any healing process, it remains essential for continued balance and protection in a chaotic, challenging, and often anxiety-ridden world.

In this book, I am going to share with you everything that I've learned both personally and professionally about what loving yourself really entails, why it's hugely advantageous to do so, and what steps you can take, both mentally and practically, to ensure that you become your own best friend and ally in this challenging but beautiful world. We're going to begin with some foundation building chapters designed to help you recognise what we're up against, before we move on to supplying you with some practical strategies to ditch your shame and reclaim your greatness! Welcome. There's a fascinating journey ahead for you even if I do say so myself.

We're going to start at the beginning...the very beginning...

Chapter One – Original Innocence

When you came into this world you were a floppy, hungry, pooping, vomiting, crying bundle of joyful potential. In some respects, your future was already mapped out for you. Your DNA and genetics already contained the codes which would dictate how you would look, your emotional disposition, your natural intelligence level, and indeed whether you might have a propensity towards becoming a murderous psychopath or the next Mother Teresa. That's **nature**.

Then we have **nurture**. There is enough data available now to be absolutely certain that how people turn out in life is dependent upon both nature and nurture. It's not one or the other, it's both. Our first years are extremely important in this regard. To cut a long story short, if we're neglected, abused, or poorly trained in early life, we'll grow up with bad programming. This is extremely difficult to shake off, and it will create ongoing difficulties in managing life's complexities. Studies show that many people have potentially psychopathic genes but that most murderous psychopaths experienced abuse and neglect in their formative years – in case you were wondering. That tells us a lot right there.

At the core of a person is their sense of **self**. When you think about yourself, what do you feel? If the answer to this question is anything less than okay, then trust me when I say that things not only could be better for you but they **should** be better for you. Now, "should" is a dirty word. In therapeutic understanding, the word "should" can cause all kind of problems, including making you feel like the gum on someone's shoe. If you believe you should be better than you are, then you're not going to feel very good about yourself, are you? Just occasionally though, a should is a should because it needs to be. Let's suppose you just accidentally sawed your pinky-finger off with your electric breadknife. My advice would be to get that nub on ice and get yourself and your appendage to the emergency room pronto (sorry for the image). In other words, you **should** get it sewn back on. That's a clean should. When I say that your sense of self should be better than less than okay, I mean it in exactly the same way. Being at war with ourselves is no less of an injury than a severed finger. Actually, it's worse. Don't be willing to settle for anything less than okay!

I have a lot of experience in helping people to work through their resistance to being a friend to themselves. I mean it seems simple enough doesn't it? Why not just be nice to yourself and have a harmonious day? Well, unfortunately, the human psyche can get pretty messed up, especially when those early years weren't supportive, and we can carry around all sorts of beliefs which make us feel bad about ourselves as a result of those unhelpful messages from childhood. That's before we've understood the burden that evolution, culture, and other people have imposed upon us too. It's going to be very difficult to be a friend to yourself if you believe that you're not worth liking, so we need to go all the way back to the beginning to commence our journey.

One of the greatest questions ever posed to me was this: -

"Who were you before your heart got broken?"

Deep contemplation of this question has the potential to lead us to some fairly profound understandings. Please stop reading for a moment, close your eyes, and ask yourself that question. Then pay attention to where it leads you. Who were you before your heart got broken?

Interesting huh? You will probably have found that you have to go way back to answer it, possibly even before you have any conscious memory. People often speak of terrible events in their lives as if the event split their lives in two. There was who you were before the event, and who you are today. Your original innocence is who you were before your heart was broken.

Heartbreak is an unavoidable part of life. The good news is that most of the time our heartbreak eventually heals, and when we put a positive spin on our wounding, we can even say that it has made us what we are today through the wisdom and transformation that suffering brings.

Undoubtedly, experiencing suffering can help us to develop greater empathy and wisdom. It comes at a price though. Each time we are wounded, we may become a little more fearful, and a little more guarded.

This in itself is not a bad thing. While the notion of living a life with a truly open heart is a beautiful idea, in practice it is beyond the reach of most mere mortals, and potentially extremely hazardous to health. We learn quickly that open hearts are often callously stomped upon, and as a result we become more discerning about who we open up to and how much of ourselves we're willing to reveal when we do so. This is normal and healthy. Problems arise however when our hearts become so guarded that they become a fortress.

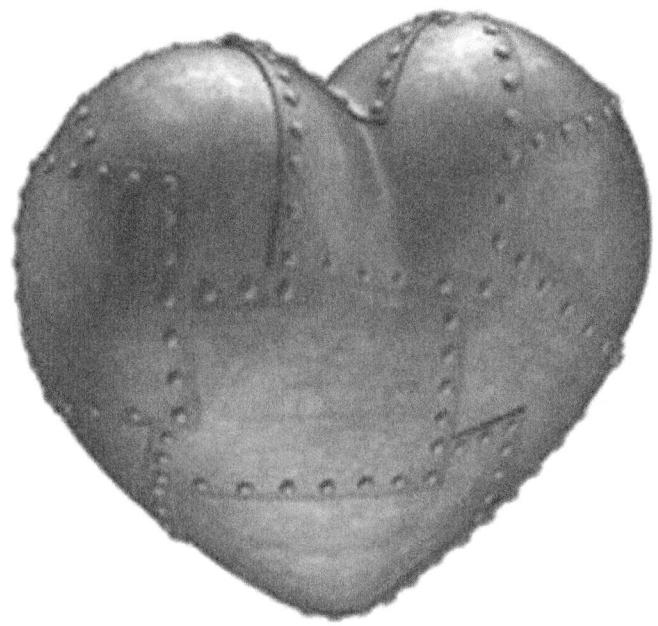

It is a sad fact of life that most of us have to deal with earth-shattering difficulty at some point or another; breakup, bereavement, loss, illness, accidents, trauma, betrayal, abuse, or breakdown. The inevitable outcome is that we are forever changed by such events. There is no going back. There is only forwards and it takes time to heal. The question which is posed to us when such events enter our lives though asks us **how** we will heal?

If you break a bone and you don't have it reset into its correct position, it will still heal but it will heal crooked. Your body will contort into unusual positions as it works to adjust every other part of your anatomy to compensate for that crooked bone. You'll get by but you'll be out of shape and possibly disabled to some degree.

Your psyche is no different. It will develop new strategies to compensate for your wound, and in practice, this means that you're working much harder to deal with life than you would if your original-self had remained unchanged. When a broken bone is properly set and allowed to heal correctly, the bones are not only knitted together at the molecular level but the body also places extra bone around the break area to reinforce it. The break point is stronger than it was prior to the injury.

In a perfect world then, we'd design our healing process deliberately to ensure that we heal stronger, and indeed, there's a reason that we say "what doesn't kill you only makes you stronger". Often it does but some wounds don't receive the benefit of being set correctly, and they heal crooked. Of particular note here then, are the injuries we may have sustained in early life. As an adult you have a much wider range of methods, experience, and resources available to you to design your healing process so that you heal right. As a very tiny human being however, no such tools are available. Your wounds heal exactly as they are, and this right here is the early core of a poor sense of self.

As you grew into your new shoes your body developed just like everyone else's but inside you may have felt different. You were "crooked". Nobody could see this but you knew it was there. Something wasn't right. It was worse than that. Something was **wrong** with you, and despite your best efforts to fit in and smile easily, this feeling persisted. If you were lucky, you made good friends and it went away for a while but when you were alone or in trouble it was always there, pecking away at you like a hen on steroids, relentlessly reminding you that if something went wrong, then it was **your** fault.

If you're reading this book, there's a good chance that it's still there...still reminding you that everything that hurts in life is because there's something wrong with you. It tells you that when bad things happen it's because you're flawed, and it tells you not to bother trying to achieve anything of value, because you're a failure. If you do succeed in something, you're told it was just luck and won't happen again. It has many other unfriendly messages for you too, and we'll be getting to those in detail shortly but before we do, let's set a few things straight.

At this point, if you were nodding along to the last paragraph, then what I'm about to tell you is likely to be meaningful for you consciously but you may well struggle to believe that these rules apply to you too. As always, I want this book to reach you at the deepest level possible, meaning that I recognise that just because something makes sense, we can still find enormous resistance within ourselves to taking it on board so that it becomes a living truth. Don't worry. We expect that at this point. For now, I just want to present you with a little bit of logic which can set the scene for us.

So, here's the truth. **You are the way you are because of four central factors.** There are others but I want to focus on these for now.

* **One** - The first of these is your DNA and genetics. As far as we can know, you didn't choose your body. You got what you got and then you've had to work with that. This includes the talents and limitations present within your family line, and it also includes the evolutionary programming present within Humanity as a whole.

* **Two** - The second is your upbringing. You were powerless to influence how your caregivers treated you, and therefore powerless to choose what effect that treatment and/or training would have upon your adaptation to life.

* **Three** - The third is your environment. You were also powerless to do much about this, and it had **everything** to do with what chance you had of making a success of life.

* **Four** - The fourth is your life experience. Stuff happens, and some of what has happened has left you at a disadvantage. You have always done the best you knew how to do with the resources available to you at any given time. Those resources were a direct result of one, two, and three.

Think about it clearly. **There is cause and effect.**

To summarise clearly then, you are not the way you are solely because of the choices you have made in your life. You are very much a product of your genetic line, your upbringing, your environment, and other people's choices too, many of which took place long before you were even born.

If there are any (perceived) inadequacies in your being, have you considered that you may not have been dealt a fair hand? I'm not suggesting that we make victims of ourselves or abdicate responsibility. I'm just being the voice of reason for a moment. Not everything in your life has been within your control, and it's very important to begin this journey with that understanding in place. You're going to need some leverage when it comes to unlearning your negative feelings and thoughts about yourself. This is the first tool in your toolbox.

If "cause and effect" isn't a good enough reason to cut yourself some slack, there's another factor which is so overlooked that it's almost taboo. If you know my story, then you'll know that the following words marked a turning point in my life. Here they are:

Life Is Difficult.

Now, as a therapist it's my job to keep us positively focussed. If we all stumbled around each day pouting and groaning about how hard life is, planet Earth would look like an episode of The Walking Dead. We might think life is hard when we have to drag ourselves out of bed after only four hours sleep, or when the kids are playing up, or the boss is being a jerk but I'd like to invite you to take another look at those three little words with your philosophical head on.

Please forgive me for this **very brief** spell of negativity but it's entirely necessary to make the point I'm getting to. Here's why life is hard: -

* There is no instruction manual, and the human race has frequent disagreements about the rules (morality), and how they should be enforced.

* We all know without question that we are going to die, and so is everyone we know and love.

* Not only are we responsible for ourselves but we frequently have to be responsible for others too.

* Everything we have worked to build and accrue will eventually no longer belong to us.

* We experience regular physical illnesses, some minor, some catastrophic, **all** painful.

* We feel some measure of pain every single day and are completely driven by discomfort and insecurity, whether that be hunger, tiredness, needing the loo, being wet, cold, hot, thirsty, upset, filled with worry or grief, or feeling just plain unsettled and needy for no good reason at all.

* We can suffer from mental illnesses like anxiety, depression, OCD etc, all of which are torturous, and mostly involuntary.

* Most of us are under enormous pressure to make enough money to survive, and are often forced by circumstances to endure conditions which are deeply unpleasant and hurtful in various ways.

* Relating to the rest of the world is extremely complicated. We need a PHD in eye contact, voice control, body language, articulation and diplomacy just to function without it being an ordeal. Luckily, most of us get the hang of it but when you examine all of the subtleties of harmonious communication, there's no denying that it's easy to get it wrong.

* We live for eighty years on average. That's a lot of joy but it's also a lot of heartache and pain to endure. We're amazingly resilient but these things take a toll on us. That gets wearing.

* Suffering, whatever form it takes is real. The world is sometimes so difficult, that it is more than some can bear. Unfortunately, sometimes people are driven to end their lives as a result. That's a reminder of just **how** hard life is sometimes.

* There are many extremely dangerous people in the world who wish to do harm to others. Almost everyone experiences being on the receiving end of this malice at some point in their lives.

* Many painful situations are simply impossible to resolve (immediately) and outside of our control.

* Our planet faces catastrophe.

* Most of our leaders are visionless.

I could go on. I'm sure you could add a few too. So, let's agree then that life **is** hard? It's incredibly hard.

If you're in a human body, doing a human life, trust me, you're a freaking hero!

In one of my spiritual fantasies (stay with me here rationalists, just a quick detour), I see myself arriving in the afterlife to a rapturous applause and cheering as my light-bodied Kin welcome me home. There are high fives and celebrations. "Man, you did a human life…you're a Legend! Hardly anyone dares to do an Earth life. That's like the most extreme experience you can have!" And I'm not just talking about myself. I could imagine that everyone receives this treatment as they float back to the light, because from a spiritual point of view (no nervous system and basically made of light and consciousness), this physical life would be like running the gauntlet. It's a fantasy, and maybe a childish one at that but the way I see it, if it isn't like that, well in a fair universe it **would** be, because however we got here, it actually is that challenging when all things are considered, and in my opinion we each deserve a medal.

So, what's my point? Original innocence? It's very simple. The game isn't rigged in our favour. This isn't just a spiritual issue either. It's about evolution, and we'll be understanding this in the next chapter. If we can look at these facts squarely **without making victims of ourselves** in the process, then we can take a carefully considered position on our right to feel worthy in life. Since being at war with ourselves is underpinned by harsh self-judgement, isn't it in fact reasonable to ask whether we're being fair-minded in our self-judgements, under these challenging circumstances? Indeed, are we being fair to each other in our judgements?

Self-love isn't fashionable but judging seems to be. Have you seen what fills our media and magazine racks? You may not have noticed but you are encouraged to be hard on yourself. I hear those Women's magazines are harsh! Does that sound like a good plan for happiness to you?

The question, "Who were you before your heart got broken?", is the question which leads me back to the understanding I need to find peace within myself. At the beginning of my life I was a beautiful open-hearted little boy who just wanted to love and be loved. Then things got complicated. It is the way things are but it's not my fault personally that things are complicated. They just are. Why blame myself? Complication is not my doing. It is the world I have been born into.

I am a man now. I will be forty-seven years young this year. I have a fully developed adult self, and like I said, myself and I are buddies. Together we've got a fair slice of the chaos under some measure of control. I do identify strongly with the composite of personality who has developed throughout my adult life but he's not primary. I recognise that the person I was before life forced me to close down certain parts of myself is the real me, the **whole** me, maybe even the **angelic** me?

Much as it may seem that we've spent our lives adding to ourselves, it's actually quite the opposite. Sure, maybe you've accrued wealth and possessions, skills and accolades but if you think about it carefully, you'll recognise that you've had to censor yourself ruthlessly to fit in; to be what's expected of you. You've built a personality which works well enough to get by. There's nothing wrong with this, we have to do so but if you identify **primarily** with that personality alone, you're overlooking your most wonderful asset.

What is that asset? That's the sweetness of your open heart which wants nothing more than to simply love and be loved. That's the person whose greatest joy in life is to share a moment of sweetness with another. That is who you truly are, and when you choose to **ultimately** identify with that version of yourself, you will recognise that you are an innocent, because that's the **essence**, the original, open, loving-hearted version of who you really are. It's who you would **still** be if life wasn't filled with peril, poor programming, scarcity, and heartbreak which has forced you to vie for position and protect yourself in ways that you wouldn't have chosen if you'd had a choice. If life was filled with love, sweetness, ease and comfort, you can be sure that you would be beautiful and radiant in every way. It isn't though.

So…

You didn't stop being that sweetness because you were flawed. You stopped being that because the world is flawed. You remain essentially innocent. This is your original innocence.

Chapter Two – Monkeys And Angels

There are worse fates in the world than not feeling good enough, and as feelings go, this is rarely the most extreme in terms of intensity but it is definitely among the worst of feelings in terms of its yucky-ness. Feeling like you're fundamentally unworthy of existence is utterly depressing at best and unbearably painful at worst.

It might surprise you to know that a very high proportion of people don't feel good enough, however well they hide it. Rest assured, we all suffer from a bit of it. The reasons for this are many and varied but there are a number of principal areas which need to be explored right away in order to understand how and why we can be constantly plagued by these awful feelings, and why they are essentially lying to us. We are going to kick off then with the role that evolution is playing in creating feelings of continual lack of worth within us.

Consider that human beings are pack animals who have lived together in small groups, usually numbering less than one hundred and fifty

members, historically speaking. In such small groups each member of the community would have a somewhat intimate connection with every other member of the group. In other words, everyone would know each other and there would be no way of hiding one's flaws.

At one level, we are primates, and that means that our species gravitates towards a hierarchical structure of social organisation, with an Alpha (dominant member) at the head of the group. We still do. We have "leaders", and they're often surprisingly tall, with intimidating presences.

Within our social groups, we are programmed to seek out the fittest, smartest, healthiest, and most attractive mates, in order to ensure that mating produces a strong line of descendants. This is purely Nature at work. If you can be one of the fit, smart, healthy, attractive members of the group, you can relax. You're automatically desirable which means that you're safe, and your membership and status within the group is assured. If you're not fabulous though, there's a possibility of being left behind. That's stressful and it bothers us greatly.

Our animal bodies are programmed therefore to be in competition with each other, as well as in co-operation with each other. This makes for a very complicated picture as far as our emotional selves are concerned. On the one hand, it is necessary that there are bonds of love within a human group in order to protect the groups' existence as a whole but when it comes to individual units within the group, there will be competition as each member vies for a secure position within the hierarchy. Humanity pulls together beautifully in times of war but attacks itself in peace time.

One of the worst fates that an early human being could endure within such a small group, would be to be ostracized. This would almost certainly spell the end of life for such an individual, because survival, historically speaking, has always needed to be a team effort. It goes without saying that life is programmed to survive, so when survival is threatened, anxiety and tension are the natural result. Anxiety and tension are Nature's signal to us as individuals that there is a threat in the environment, and that something needs to be done in order to eliminate the danger.

The next worst fate within the small group is to be among the weakest members. We could imagine that the weaker members of the group would be relegated to all of the most miserable tasks, receiving only the food which other members are not willing to eat, and may possibly even be socially shunned and bullied by the stronger members. Sadly, we see shades of this behaviour still very much in evidence within our species today – the haves and have nots. However, as a collective, we have been slowly working on making improvements in these areas and most of us are now in agreement that we need to provide the most vulnerable members of our group (society) with additional help, care, and security. Nonetheless, we must remember that we have this animal programming to be competitive amongst ourselves, very much alive within us, and there are members of our community who embrace survival of the fittest as their core moral code.

In practice, this means that we carry a great deal of tension about being seen as worthy and valuable within the group. Nature has provided us with an inbuilt sense that we are fundamentally "not good enough" in order to ensure that we don't become complacent as a member of the group. Competition is good for evolution. We are programmed to prove ourselves so that the other members of the group will see our value, and we will be assured of our social standing within the hierarchy, thus avoiding the unpleasant fates outlined above.

This feeling of not being good enough is also designed to be **persistent.** A hierarchy operates as a fluid system. It's not the case that you achieve your rank and that's it for the rest of your days. A fall from grace could come at any moment. In nature we see regular challenges by the stronger members of the group to the authority and dominance of the Alpha at the head of the group. It's not easy being the boss. Hostile takeovers are never far away.

A little lower down in the hierarchy, smaller battles continue to rage. If a member becomes complacent and fails to perform to a reasonable standard, then naturally, their ranking within the group will diminish. Keep that up for too long and you'll soon find yourself relatively powerless. If you understand this clearly enough then, you will also understand why no matter how well you are doing in life, you may still not feel good enough. Feeling like you should always be better than you are is a part of your evolutionary programming, and it is literally millions of years old, so you might as well give up on any hopes of that feeling ever being completely absent from your experience of life. An individual cannot generally override such deep instincts in a single lifetime.

If that sounds like bad news to you, let me reassure you that it really doesn't need to be. We may not be able to completely switch the feeling off but that doesn't mean that we have to live with it as if it were true. **We can choose to disregard the message.**

It's important to recognise that this is one of the central obstacles which we all face equally when considering why we might feel negatively about ourselves emotionally. If this programming were not understood, then it would be very easy to feel the feelings and believe that they must say something about who we are. In fact, it's much more accurate and helpful to feel these feelings and recognise them as the natural outcome of two million years' worth of primate evolution. They really don't say very much about you at all. Everybody experiences these sensations, and the trick is to be able to bring them into the light of awareness and see them for what they really are, without believing that they are meaningful within the context of modern life.

They can now be viewed as an evolutionary hangover. We no longer live in small groups as a rule, and in the developed world, we generally have enough abundance now that we no longer need to fight for our position to physically survive. We still have a way to go socially before everyone is properly cared for but few of us are truly at risk of death if we get it wrong. There's usually some social system to catch us when we fall too low. Our emotional intelligence and intellectual understanding has developed more quickly than our programming though. The level of anxiety that some of us can feel around not good enough-ness can be attributed to the fact that being good enough once really was a matter of life or death. It was relevant then but it isn't any more. I believe that we are literally in the process now of updating that programming, and I'll tell you more later on about why I hold this belief.

It's entirely possible that by reading this book, or implementing any other resource which helps you towards healing and well-being, you will, in some strange and mysterious way, be contributing to the new programming that your descendants will receive. This may sound like an inflated statement but don't you think it is strange that we can now hand an iPad to a two- year old child and they will have mastered it within a month? I'm quite sure that if you had given me an iPad at two years of age I would simply have smashed it with my wooden hammer. So where are these two-year olds getting their understanding from? Why don't they also throw the device against the wall and smash it to smithereens?

It seems to me that the most obvious answer is that familiarity with new information is embedded (learned) and passed on to the next generation.

In essence, their parents have been using iPads for the last ten or fifteen years, and at some deep level, this recognition and understanding has programmed their DNA. When they then go on to have children, that understanding is passed on with the DNA. (The science of epigenetics in psychology is here http://noba.to/37p5cb8v for interested parties.) Then, the object is not unfamiliar. Intuitively, instinctively, the child knows exactly what that object is for and what you are supposed to do with it. It is debateable though, so I'll just call it a proposal.

It is also likely that the rate at which we are absorbing new understanding and information into our species has been accelerating at breakneck speed throughout our most recent history. Is it then, so outlandish, to suggest that by changing ourselves psychologically today we will enable more permanent psychological change within a few generations? It seems reasonable enough to me, and it seems highly likely that this process has been underway for a very long time already. My generation, born in the 1970s, clearly have understandings beyond the reach of our parents' or grandparents' generation. I have no doubt that the generations being born today will be capable of much greater achievements than my own. Will our monkey body instincts be with us in the same form that they are today long into the future? Who can say? Our present moment is unprecedented.

For now, though, we are stuck with an evolutionary hangover. The monkey wants you to feel bad about yourself. It is our job to understand that this inherent lack of worth is involuntarily present within our bodies and minds, and then ensure that we factor this influence in when assessing for ourselves whether we deserve to feel ok about who we are.

In other words, we now have the sufficient understanding necessary to tell the monkey mind to "do one!" (that's UK slang for "go away!"), and start working towards remembering that there's something which looks a lot like an angel within each one of us too.

Chapter Three – Let's Talk About Parents

If monkeys are **nature**, then parents and caregivers are the first stop on the **nurture** trail. Let's not pretend that Humanity's journey through time has been easy. A rose-tinted view of our ancestors' "at one with Nature and blissfully connected" lives would be inaccurate. Many hells have undoubtedly been repeatedly endured. It's a scientific fact that the planet has been through ten ice ages during Humanity's evolution.

One thing that we can be certain of though is that when humans lived in small groups, the children were cared for. There are many animal species' who abandon their young at birth. Primates are not one of them.

Bear in mind that we have spent over 99% of our evolutionary time on planet Earth living in hunter-gatherer societies consisting of a small number of people. Kit Opie, an evolutionary anthropologist from University College London tells us that "The modern monogamous culture has only been around for just 1,000 years". In our early ancestral cultures, polyamorous sexual practice was common. As a result, nobody knew for sure who fathered the children. In a way then, the children born were "everybody's" children and naturally the role of parenting then fell upon the group as a whole rather than just a single pair of parents.

Concern for the children has always been primary. If the children didn't survive, then the group would die out. Child mortality rates were extremely high in ancestral life so every child was considered precious and valued, and cared for as an absolute priority. Most importantly, caring for the children was a **group** priority. As a result, no child would be neglected. Tens of thousands of generations of such experience have programmed us right down to the core of our being to **expect** to be cared for. In addition to this, we have historically enjoyed the protection and influence of many individuals during our formative years, which would naturally lead to a good balance of skills and perspectives, as well as a strong overall sense of community and safety (despite the later "ranking" issues).

Now you get just the two parents. If you're lucky, you might be born to an extended family too. There are pros and cons to this modern arrangement, and when it works well it can produce well-adjusted healthy adults but since we have transitioned from extended tribe to small family unit, some perversions have developed. Closed doors have given permission for some of the darker traits of Humanity to emerge without the balancing influences of the group to either notice, or assist, with healing.

Community has given way to insular familial environments, and in some cases, wounds have festered within family lines. Unhealed wounds are a menace to well-being. They obstruct peace and make it difficult, if not impossible, to function in a streamlined and harmonious way. We get by because we have to but wounding is like a boulder in a stream. The water can flow around it but the flow is constricted and urgent. At a psychological level, wounds require that people develop strategies to flow around the obstacle, which is another way of saying that they might think and behave in compromised ways. That's being polite. In plain English terms it might mean that they are completely unfit to be a parent.

If you are unlucky enough to be born into such a family, your chances of growing up unscathed are not good. People who have not been valued, or worse still, actively abused in their own upbringings, often lack the understanding of what constitutes love. Even with the best intentions therefore, they may fail as parents themselves.

As a therapist I have always been mindful when working on these matters with people to ensure that my clients know that we have no intention of having a "parent bashing" session. We are naturally inclined to be protective towards our parents even if they were negligent or misguided in their efforts but we must not allow this sentimentality to obscure the facts. If you didn't get what you needed in your upbringing, you need to be brave enough to acknowledge this fact squarely. This is not the same as hating on your parents. Do be aware that there is a distinction.

Ultimately, these tales of family wounding being passed down from one generation to the next are often tragedies. Somewhere along the line, somebody didn't get what they needed, and as a result they became broadly incapable of meeting the emotional needs of their own offspring. Where this is the case, it's compassionate to recognise that our parents might have tried their best with what they had, and give them the due credit. In other words, you can love your parents but still recognise that you were under-served by them. This doesn't need to be an inner conflict. It just is what it is. Those are the facts. Could the parents have tried harder? Maybe? Maybe not. Every case is different.

In some cases, parents are wilfully ignorant, neglectful, or abusive. Some parents are just plain irresponsible and selfish. You can be sure that this is also a case of wounding but where should we draw the line with our compassion and understanding? Did your parents choose to find mercy in themselves for you, despite their own pain? Could they? I don't know the answer to those questions. Maybe a visit to a therapist was in order? Maybe they needed to pick up a few books? Maybe their pain was so deep that they just couldn't bring themselves to deal with it? Or maybe they were just lazy and nasty?

We really can't know for sure why some people are the way that they are but we do know that some people **appear** to choose dysfunction. If you are the son or daughter of such parents, let's remember, that even if you choose to hold them in your heart with understanding and forgiveness, you owe it to yourself at least equally, to remember that they were poor at their job. Don't make excuses for them. They failed you. They had a job to do. They didn't do it. Those are the facts.

Many children watch their parents self-destruct. It's tragic in itself but an even greater tragedy is that the children of such parents can be left with the unshakeable certainty that it is somehow their own fault. This can be crushing in two ways. Firstly, a child may feel that it is their responsibility to rescue their parents. Secondly, they may conclude that their parents' incomprehensible behaviour is because of something they said, did, or are. If it's the latter, we're in big trouble. The message then is that **"I am not good enough"**. In an effort to "save" their parents and ultimately gain self-validation in the process, a child in this situation will enter into gargantuan soul-destroying efforts to make the situation right. Why? They are programmed to do so by ten thousand generations who went before them. This programming tells them that the expected format of guaranteed care is not being followed. They are supposed to receive it but they are not getting it. Using evolutionary and child logic, there can only be one reason: -

There must be something wrong with me.

Can they succeed in fixing the situation? No. They can't win because the problem is not with them. The failure is with the parents but that will not stop them trying. With every attempt to fix it (be validated and attended to), they will conclude over and over again that the failing is their own, compounding the sense that they're not good enough until it is all that they know. This is a crushing experience, and the results of such an upbringing usually has lasting effects because this powerful sense of being fundamentally unworthy of existence will be instilled at the core level of that person's programming.

This is an awful story but a necessary one to tell because until this is recognised, we stand little chance of reclaiming the self-worth which is our **birth right**.

You should have received a very different message, and if you didn't get it at that time, let me be the first to say that I'm here standing up for your absolute right to reclaim your sense of self-worth **now**. Your sense of self-worth is absolutely primary and fundamental to your existence as a human being. Without it you will have a very difficult time being a successful and decent human being, and if you do succeed despite the handicap, it will only be because you have been working ten times as hard as you would otherwise have needed to. This is the legacy of your loss. It's time to get serious about reclaiming what is rightfully yours.

One point, worth noting here, is that this is not an invitation to make victims of ourselves. Yes, we want to recognise that we may have been under-served but we don't ever want that to become an explanation for why we can't adjust to life. Most of us have inherited wounding of one kind or another. Our job is to transcend this, not wallow in it. Don't sweat on this right now. We'll be moving on to solutions once we've explored what we are up against.

Chapter Four – Self-Esteem Versus Self-Worth

One distinction which is very important to understand is that of self-esteem versus self-worth. It helps to begin by defining what "esteem" means. Esteem, essentially means, being held in high regard. People, professions, and achievements of note are commonly held in high esteem. Self-esteem is the regard with which you hold yourself.

In order to understand the distinction between the two, it's necessary to consider what it means to be alive from two different perspectives. On the one hand, life gives birth to itself. Alan Watts once said that as a tree produces apples, so the Earth produces people. In fact, it would be more accurate to say that the Earth produces everything. Nonetheless, we can see ourselves as an extension of life. We are not separate from it. **We are it.**

Life is primarily programmed to survive and ultimately develop and thrive. If you are spiritually minded, you might call this God in a state of becoming. If you're scientifically minded or atheistic in your beliefs, then you would just call it nature and evolution. The distinction is almost irrelevant because the fact is that life is pro-life. I'm not talking here about abortion issues. When I say pro-life, I mean **for** life. This means that at a fundamental level life believes in life, if not in a minded way literally, then certainly in a practical way. Life generally nurtures itself. Even though it feeds on itself, the intention is to keep going. If you think this through carefully, the logical conclusion is that life values itself.

By definition then, if life values itself, it must also have worth. You, as a human being are a part of that life, and therefore are born with an <u>inherent</u> sense of self-worth.

There is no question that our self-worth is affected by the experiences and the valuing that we receive throughout our lives, but the basic biological drive to survive and thrive contains within it the instruction that you have value.

In short, to reiterate my earlier point, a sense of self-worth is your birth right, and despite the contradictory message from the evolutionary primate programming that you're not good enough, life itself (capital letters - LIFE) will encourage you to cherish your sense of self-worth until the day that you die, because having inherent value is your true nature as a part of life.

Somehow many of us have arrived at the erroneous conclusion that self-worth is a luxury. Nothing could be further from the truth. We need to recognise that such an idea is distorted. The relevance of this cannot be overstated. If you are to reclaim your sense of self-worth, you're going to require a sense of determination, but beyond that, you're also going to need to know right down to the very core of who you are, that it is the right thing to do. I hope I have made a clear case here for precisely why it is yours to reclaim.

The second point of view which needs to be considered, is that a proportion of your sense of self-value relates directly to your standing within the social system, your achievements, your behaviours, and your sense of morality. In other words, how highly you are regarded, that is, your reputation. How others see you is social-esteem. How you see yourself is self-esteem.

Self-esteem is quite different from self-worth. Self-worth is a given. It is not earned. It's already deposited in your bank account by LIFE when you arrive on Earth. It is what life gives you to get you started, and it's what's left when everything else has been stripped away.

Self-esteem however can be considered the deposits that you make into that bank account as a result of your efforts in life. Self-esteem is a luxury. Self-esteem is what you earn. Self-esteem is conditional. It can be gained and it can be lost.

If you are in possession of self-worth, it is not necessary to have a high level of esteem to feel good about what you are.

Esteem is nice to have. It makes the ego happy. It also secures your position in the social hierarchy. Human beings often make a very costly mistake here. Without an understanding of this distinction, a person can easily decide that their sense of value about themselves rests entirely on esteem, as opposed to self-worth. Self-esteem is driven by the ego, and the problem with the ego is that it is fundamentally insatiable in its appetites for approval and recognition. The pursuits of the ego can lead us into a quest for greater admiration from other people, the acquisition of unnecessary wealth, and a high status within the social system. In other words, being a winner, being cool.

If you are lucky enough to be one of the cool kids, that is, having a fantastic personality, financial success, a beautiful house, a great body, good looks, and everybody thinks you're wonderful, that's really nice. I'm pleased for you. No sarcasm intended. That's a nice life and who wouldn't want it? But what happens if you lose it all? Where's your foundation? If your entire sense of your value rests on what you have accumulated or achieved, rather than what you **are**, then you're on thin ice, aren't you? That's not a strong position should the big bad wolf come calling.

The problem with self-esteem then, is that it is utterly conditional. What this means in practice is that those people who feel badly about themselves will often fall into the trap of deciding that they feel bad because they need more validation, more recognition, more achievements, more possessions, and better social status. This translates broadly as the conditional statement "I can **only** feel ok about myself once I have achieved X status."

Self-worth, by comparison, will still be there if you become destitute.

The sad truth is that some folks will never achieve those dizzying heights of achievement or acclaim. The higher the bar is set of course, the more out of reach any sense of self-worth will be. The most damaging aspect of this trap is that people can use up their entire lifetimes reaching for this imagined perfection, run themselves into the ground, and lead utterly awful lives as a result.

Those who do achieve their desired status within life as a means to feel "good enough", often find the experience deeply disappointing because "good enough" is not something to be achieved. It's something you **are**. The journey is one of uncovering, remembering, recognition, and reclaiming, not achievement.

Chapter Five – A Surprising Revelation

Many years ago, I walked into a therapist's consulting room with a strong feeling that I was about to be mauled. I'd been desperately ill for the last six or seven years with severe anxiety and depression, and my pride had been ripped to shreds. I really had nothing left to lose. I fully expected to be judged. The therapist would hide it well, I thought, but it was my own fault, and we'd both know it. I'd brought it upon myself, and I deserved everything I got. That, at least, was the subconscious agenda playing out in my feeling body. In my conscious mind, I was still clinging to the idea that what was left of me was a nice guy. I didn't deserve the inhumane level of torture I'd endured. I hadn't done any harm to anyone, despite my illness, and I definitely gave 110% every single day. In my estimation that meant that I must still like myself.

My unconscious mind had another agenda altogether. You see, I'd made some terrible errors of judgement in my life seven years previously, which had resulted in a trauma so shocking that it was genuinely doubtful whether I could come back from it. Every time I had tried to get up and live my life like a normal human being, I'd been slapped down hard, and then kicked some more. It was a relentless beating, merciless, and brutal, and I blamed life. In some ways this was accurate. Life can be brutal sometimes.

I've spoken about this in detail elsewhere so I'll keep it short and to the point. I'd never found therapists to be uncaring or disinterested but neither had I ever experienced what was about to happen. This lady sat me down and looked right through my pain. You see, she already knew something that I didn't yet. My self-esteem was literally non-existent. As far as I was concerned, I'd completely failed at life. I'd broken myself, possibly irretrievably. I'd become useless as a husband to my ever loving but unable to help wife, and I was frankly, waiting to die, and hoping that it would come sooner rather than later so that this nightmare could end. But she barely cared about any of that. She was looking right into my eyes and pushing past all that stuff, probing, barely even listening to what I was saying, and then she found it...she found **me**. I was buried in there, and somehow, she got through. It was a "pow!" moment. I saw her see me, and it was mind-blowing. I hadn't even known I was still there! I thought he was dead, gone, obliterated, finished - no more!

How did she do it? She **knew** he was still there. I had given up on him. Moreover, she didn't only know that he was still there but she knew that the reason I had failed to heal, was precisely because he hadn't been reclaimed. That was her mission, and she knew it from the moment I set foot in that consulting room. I cannot describe the sense of relief which came over me. I knew then that this hopeless nightmare could end. I knew it would still be a long road ahead. I didn't expect a miracle but for the first time in years, something significant had happened, and I had hope again. I'd been waiting a long time for this but I hadn't known what "this" would be until it happened.

This last surviving part of myself, that she found, was my intrinsic value, my "worth". Despite all that I'd been through, a living hell no less, he had survived.

She reactivated him by seeing him...and then believing in him.

She understood that this was the foundation from which I could re-build myself because she understood what his true nature was. He was not hate or hurt, disappointment, or fear. He was my original innocence. He was literally bent out of shape by the weight of the debris which had crushed my heart over the years but he was alive, and she knew that with healing, he could remember who he really was...**what** he really was.

At that point, I still had a way to go yet though. He was not happy about what had happened over the last seven years. He'd been skipping along, merrily enjoying existence, when some idiot (namely me!) had decided to go off on some extreme mission which brought the whole house down in a terrifying implosion of rubble and mortar. I'd been weeping and wounded in the devastation ever since, and he had been buried, presumed dead, for seven long years. He had every right to be mad at me. Goodness knows I had been mad at myself.

So that is how I began my journey towards loving myself. It may not begin with niceties. Often it will begin with deep self-estrangement. The spiritual Alchemists of old used to say, "The darker, the better", that is, the deeper the wounding, the more thorough the healing will ultimately be. Over the years I've taken great comfort from many myths and allegories which have described the process of transformation in metaphor quite perfectly. Once the process is understood, you begin to see this transformational structure repeated in our most beloved stories. It's no accident that fiction emulates life. The story of the hero looks something like this: -

Act One – Departure.

The ordinary world on auto-pilot. We're largely just going about our business in a relatively unconscious way. Then, in some form, there is a call to adventure. A mission presents but the hero is hesitant. An event and/or the arrival of a mentor triggers definitive action. The protagonist is filled with doubt but departs nonetheless.

Act Two – Initiation/Deep Peril/Transformation

Our hero leaves her old world behind. She steps into the unknown and meets with forces which tear her to pieces, a process of disintegration. "The Dark Night Of The Soul", a period of abandonment and terror follows, and she will ultimately face her worst fears in a series of genuinely perilous trials, in a precarious state herself. A process of death and re-birth unfolds as she dies to what she was and learns to identify with that which is immortal within her because it is only that which **can** survive this journey. She is transformed.

Act Three – Resolution and Return

She must return to her community with the gifts and lessons from her transformative journey. This is a process of re-integration as a fully alive, fully awake human being with one foot in each world. She earns her own peace by having faced the worst aspects of life (and often death), and recognizes that to contribute to the community in service is all that is left to do, thus becoming truly free to share from herself fearlessly. She has reclaimed what she truly is, she understands what is truly valuable, and she is no longer at the mercy of the ego's pursuits or the judgements of others.

"Those who know, not only that the Everlasting lies in them, but that what they, and all things, really are is the Everlasting, dwell in the groves of the wish fulfilling trees, drink the brew of immortality, and listen everywhere to the unheard music of eternal concord." – Joseph Campbell

This three-act story describes pretty perfectly what has happened to me (though I'm not sure about the eternal concord part!), and indeed it has happened to many others too. Perhaps, in some way, this is a journey that we all undertake in some shape or form throughout our lives? Ultimately, it is the story of taking our power back – re-discovering and reclaiming our true selves. Does this imply that in order to find self-love we must go on an epic journey of peril and discovery? Not at all. Rest assured that no crisis or emergency is necessary to reclaim your self-worth. I include the understanding here though for those who do find themselves in a state of confusion or angst. It's a very human experience and a well-trodden path. Have faith that it's a journey, and you **will** emerge!

The finer details of my own healing process I'll share with you as analogy later as we explore what it means to truly love yourself. For now, let's just acknowledge that this rabbit hole runs much deeper than many people know, or recognize.

Chapter Six – Your Heart Is In The Right Place

I may not know you personally but I'd be willing to bet a small amount that you do the best that you can with what you've got in life? I'd also bet that you've **always** done the best you can. You might not see it that way though. You have regrets and doubts…like *maybe I could have done more?* Well hindsight is a wonderful thing isn't it?

If you were sent back in time **without** the understanding you have accrued since those events, you would almost certainly do exactly the same thing again. I'm suggesting that it was really the only thing you could do because despite the regrettable outcomes, you **were** doing your very best. *"Ah…but was I?"* you ask yourself. With your rose-tinted specs and brutal honesty in place you are reminded that you kind of knew you were being foolish or lazy at the time. You conclude that you could have done more indeed, and that there are no excuses.

Here's the thing though. Yes, you probably did know that you weren't doing your best at the time but that was still doing your best. This sounds like gobbledygook excuses, right? Except you're not factoring in a hidden element. You were being driven in that particular moment by an incredibly complex cocktail of feelings and drives which you were almost certainly **completely unaware of consciously**. That's not something you will have had any control over. Your conscious mind might have had some awareness that you were about to make a mistake but your **unconscious** mind runs the show!

There were in fact a million micro-calculations taking place in a hidden part of your brain which made you do things the way you did them. In a single moment of decision, your brain had to piece together an astonishing number of fragments of memories and experiences. It had to juggle how you feel with what you know and what you hope for. It had to forecast an almost infinite number of possible outcomes and place a bet on the one it thought most likely, and most fruitful. It had to imagine stepping into the shoes of the people or things which would be affected, and make a judgement call on whether the cost to them would be greater than the suffering it would alleviate in you, and then decide whether that fitted with your moral obligation to yourself, others, and the world. If you were under stress at the time, then the entire decision-making process was being sabotaged by the toxic effects of stress. Are you factoring all of that in when deciding whether you did your "best"?

I'm not suggesting that we hold ourselves unaccountable for our actions. I'm saying that we cannot change what is done, and holding ourselves emotionally hostage by selling ourselves the idea that we must be poorly intentioned in life is a recipe for emotional disaster. Self-love includes self-forgiveness, and that involves cutting ourselves some slack by accurately assessing what we're up against at any given time.

What you remember as laziness was probably fear and depression. What you remember as selfishness was exhaustion. What you remember as stupidity was an appetite for adventure. It's very easy to look back in judgement and decide that you failed because you were poorly intentioned but is that accurate? You're free to disagree with me but I would argue that the things that made you do the things you did were inescapable at that particular moment. You were doing your best, and that's another way of saying "Your heart was in the right place".

Our much-loved late friend Carrie Fisher wisely said:-

"My heart is in the right place. I know it is 'cos I hid it there".

This comment is incisive. As you may know, Carrie battled with mental health difficulties throughout her life, and was a staunch advocate for speaking out against mental health stigma. By all accounts she was wise, funny, and gorgeous. Hiding one's heart is often a necessary defence mechanism in a challenging world, and it's one of the reasons that none of us should judge anyone too quickly.

People often say or do things which are not representative of their true intentions because they are operating under duress, or being otherwise affected by influences which are not obvious to the observer. So, goes the saying "Don't judge another until you have walked a mile in their shoes". To my mind, this isn't recommending that people be endlessly forgiven for malicious behaviour. Rather, it is an invitation to extend our understanding beyond knee-jerk reactions.

For instance, somebody told me a story about a megastar that they shared an elevator with. It was a scathing account of how she was so rude, and being a diva, because she didn't hold the doors open and didn't speak to them. Dude, you shared an elevator with her, not a relationship. Anything to inject some drama. I discounted the story. I'll make up my own mind about her next time we're on my yacht. (I don't have a yacht. I'll never have one. I do like to make jokes about it though).

Derren Brown recounts in his book, "Tricks of the mind", how he rushed into a café in Bristol in a flustered state, searching for a friend he was due to meet but failed to register that a couple who were leaving had held the door open for him. He unintentionally didn't acknowledge or thank them. He says "I heard a mumbling of my name and a "Did you see that? Unbelievable!" but he had missed his moment to say thank you. He went on to say that he cringes to this day, and expects that the story went viral, and all who heard it now believe he is total **** (his four-letter word). Clearly, he is actually an extraordinarily nice human being. Celebrities have to leave generous tips when they go out to eat and otherwise behave impeccably in every moment because sadly, many people are simply eager to judge. It seems that those in elevated positions in the social hierarchy make the easiest targets.

At a deeper level, sometimes people are struggling with unseen issues which may make them come across as unpleasant or inattentive. It's so easy to judge. It takes work to step back and wonder.

> **"Let us be kind to one another, for most of us are fighting a hard battle."** *(Ian MacLaren)*

So, when it comes to deciding whether your heart is in the right place or not, who's to judge you? I wouldn't recommend leaving that up to anyone else but **yourself** because aside from the fact that it's not really anyone's business but your own, something which has to be factored in when assessing whether other people's judgements are accurate or helpful, is where they themselves are coming from?

We've already established that people can make knee-jerk judgements, and if they are gossip-minded they will find fault where there is none. In addition to this though, wounded people tend to "project" their wounding onto others. If you think back to the monkey mind again, this should make sense. If there is a hierarchy, and somebody is feeling themselves to be at a dangerously low level on the "esteem" scale, they are hardly going to want to praise and raise you up, are they? That's essentially demoting themselves, and that's before we've even gotten to the jealousy part. Your success reminds them of their pain or (perceived) failure. That's enough for them to hate you right there. Your power to decide what constitutes good-heartedness is too precious to be handed to someone else.

So, it's **up to you** to decide whether your heart's in the right place or not? If you're suffering with a lack of self-love or self-worth generally, there's every chance that you're going to be rather hard on yourself in this assessment because you're probably listening to a whiny little voice which hides in your head...

The Inner Critic! Who or what is the inner-critic? Well, as the name suggests, it's the component within your personality which/who dishes out relentless self-criticism. As I acknowledged in my introduction, we need a conscience, a voice of reason, or a reminder when we're way off track. The inner critic however is not merely a conscience. It is by definition unduly negative. You see, encouragement generally bears more fruit than criticism. Criticism doesn't lift you up and show you that you're capable. It puts you down, and discourages you. The outcome of this is a complete lack of enthusiasm, which strongly reinforces the position that you're inept. Patient encouragement, by comparison, recognises that you're allowed to make mistakes as you master something.

There is no success without failure. The inner critic won't tell you that though.

The voice of the inner critic inside your head will tell you terrible things about yourself. He/She will say that you're a failure, that you're ugly, fat, useless, stupid, or nasty, and that you always will be. Sometimes it will call you four letter words.

✳ The inner critic is the monstrous voice of everyone who ever treated you poorly.

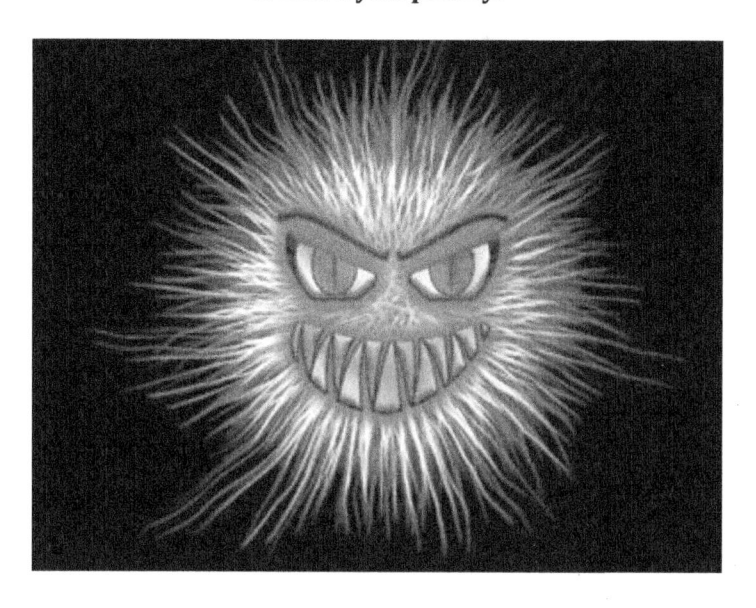

Every time you have felt rejected, unheard, abused, belittled, bullied, excluded, abandoned, shamed, or under-valued, the inner critic has been right there, vacuuming all that poison right up, and storing it in the "worthless" bank for a rainy day. Oh, it doesn't take much for this little demon to start hurling toxic darts at you, and trust me, you don't want to listen to a word of it!

We are not going to go to war with this beast in this book. We're going to make him/her irrelevant. Suffice to say that when you have got your own back, then the booming presence of the inner critic will fade to a tinny whine which can be much more easily ignored.

Chapter Seven – Morality & Hypocrisy

One of the inner critic's favourite weapons to use against you is "morality". Morality is our sense of right versus wrong, and it's a complicated area to navigate, so if we're going to stand up to the inner critic, we'll need to be nice and clear about our position.

We often hear the word "obligation" following the word moral. A "moral obligation" is another way of saying "should". There are many areas in life in which we will decide our individual moral position, and that's fine but let's begin with the simplest and most easily remembered "should" in the world.

The best measure of a balanced moral obligation is very simple: -

"Treat the world in the same way that you wish to be treated."

Or, as my friends and I like to say, "Don't be a ****!" The Pagan slogan is "Harm none, and do as you will". Nobody can argue with this, can they? Not even the inner critic. We don't need to over-complicate this. It basically means don't abuse, steal, kill, sabotage, bully, manipulate, dominate, deface, destroy or violate...wherever possible.

Beyond this, things get complicated. What's your moral position on abortion, divorce, assisted dying, animal testing, farming methods, religion, pollution, global warming, energy production, sex, genetic modification, politics, war, foreign affairs, refugees, immigration, or even taxes? If scrutinized, how many of your moral positions would be found to be in conflict with others that you hold equally dear? You get an extra star if you're completely watertight. Most of us aren't. It's a minefield.

Even following the simplest rule of harm none, it's impossible to fulfil every good intention flawlessly. You will kill millions, perhaps billions of living bacteria and germs today when you clean your kitchen or take a shower. You will tread on ants when you go for a walk. Hey, you might even deliberately swat a mosquito. You will pollute the Earth when you drive, wash your clothes, drink from a plastic bottle, or turn the TV on. The methane that comes from your bodily functions is a greenhouse gas contributing to global warming. Where do we draw the line? What makes us "bad" people? These questions, among many others, make morality a bag of unavoidable contradictions. So, let's look squarely at our situation and understand that for all our good intentions…

Hypocrisy is sometimes unavoidable.

Please do register this. Our sense of how good or bad we are, is directly linked to how closely we follow the directions of our moral compass, that is, the rules we believe we must follow. We have to know that there are many situations which make it literally impossible for us to remain squeaky clean. Don't decide that you are a bad or unworthy person because a personal moral rule gets broken. Sometimes you just can't win. That's not an excuse to abdicate all responsibility. It's simply a reason to lighten up on yourself a bit and give you some stability when dealing with a harsh inner critic, or any critic at all for that matter.

The correct position then, is to understand that this area is difficult to navigate, and then do what you can to minimise the harm you do without sacrificing yourself in the process. There's a reason that few of us get it right all the time: -

We are all works in progress.

Remember the "life is hard" part? Well that means that we are asked to meet challenges in life which stretch us to our limits at times. Under such conditions we are going to sometimes be low on energy and we are definitely going to make mistakes. Some mistakes are tiny irritating ones, and others are catastrophic life-changing ones. Most people are well-intended. Yes, I know the world has some people in it who are cruel people but **most** of us start out with good intentions. Our chaotic world would simply not function if that were not the case. There are a trillion kindnesses exchanged every day and they make the world go around. They just don't get reported very often.

Having your heart in the right place simply means being well-intentioned. We need to recognize that being human is a guaranteed experience of imperfection. The Buddhists call it "ten thousand lifetimes of dissatisfaction". Psychological research tells us that we will, on average, make the same mistake seven times before we do something differently. Obviously big mistakes grab our attention more quickly, resulting in fewer repetitions. In short though, we are doing our best with what we have available to us, and our monkey limitations mean we often make the same mistakes repeatedly. Yes, it's annoying.

It's easy to be highly judgemental of ourselves because despite the facts, we still **want** to get everything right the first time around, and then every time thereafter. We're just programmed that way. Nonetheless, when our programming, the monkey brain, lets us down by sending us emotional messages telling us that we're no good, it's our job to send them back with a polite note that says "no thank you". If that doesn't work, we'll fight for it.

As I alluded to in my introduction, there are areas of my own personal development which continue to cause me some measure of guilt. For example, I often feel that I "should" volunteer more, give more, or be more politically active. I do what I can, and I keep the rest on the radar. There is obviously a time for knuckling down and doing what **must** be done, and life will certainly impose these circumstances upon us from time to time but it's preferable to have **some** relaxed time between these periods of intensity, to recharge at a deep level. This is how we ensure that we don't sacrifice ourselves to a moral position. There are endless moral improvements to be fulfilled but when is enough too much? Having experienced a breakdown of epic proportions in my early life as a result of having too many good intentions, I am acutely aware that for the best will in the world, I simply cannot do it all. It's not my preferred position but life has made it very clear to me that my limitations must be respected first and foremost. Self-love isn't always easy or comfortable because often our needs and limitations clash with our ideas of what our best self will look like. One incredibly helpful statement in this regard which I encourage you to memorise is this: -

The world's needs far outweigh your personal ability to supply.

If we are driven exclusively by "should", we are unlikely to ever grant ourselves permission to fully rest, and it's pretty stressful feeling like you're not living up to some arbitrary standard. There is a list as long as my arm of things I think I "should" do, and that never goes away but I have learned that it is not wise to sacrifice oneself at the *Altar Of Should*.

I've done it many times, even recently (Argh! I did it again!) It rarely works out well, and is often unsustainable because the energy required to see a "should" through to completion may be more than we have to give.

One area which requires particularly careful maintenance when it comes to "should" is the level of obligation we may feel to other people. People pleasers of the world, listen up! It's lovely to help each other out, and when the balance of give and take is fair, there's no greater pleasure.

Some people though literally don't know how to say no when they need to, and they may be equally reticent to ever ask for help when they need it. If you know that you are one of those people, the chances are that everybody else knows it too. This is not good news for you. It means that you are the first person that people come to when they need help. You're "dependable", and you're low maintenance. Maybe you even pride yourself on how self-reliant and dependable you are?

The problem is that everyone who comes to you with a request thinks that they're the only one who is leaning on you. In fact, your reputation as Dependable Bob means that you've already taken on six other projects for other people. You soon become completely overloaded with everybody else's jobs and problems, and end up with no time to live your own life. You may smile sweetly. You may even kid yourself that you're okay with this but it's not a good way to live. Your own needs will end up sacrificed for the sake of someone else's.

The truth is, when people ask you to shoulder a proportion of their burden, it may not be because you're the **only** person who could help but because you're the **easiest** person to rope in. It could be your time, your money, your energy, your attention, or your possessions which are called upon but these are all **limited** resources. Your generosity is also your loss. That's fine if you really want to give it, and can afford it but if you're giving what you haven't got because you're terrified that saying no makes you a bad person, then you're in a very vulnerable position.

Unfortunately, people with low self-worth can find themselves in a tight spot on this one. If we aren't feeling great about ourselves, one way to feel validated as worthy is to gain the appreciation of someone else. Not only may we say yes to what's asked of us but we might even go out of our way to offer our services to others. We have the best intentions, of course. We're just trying to help but then one day we realise that we've taken on way too much. We've backed ourselves into a corner and there's no way out. We end up letting someone down, and then feel even more awful about ourselves. Then, we try to fix how awful we feel by offering to help...

The problem is easily solved. We have to learn that "no" is not a dirty word, and saying no is not something to be avoided at any cost. It's nice to say yes, but the fact is, if you say no, the person making the request will need to find another solution, and they will. That's all. It doesn't say anything about you. You don't have the resources to say yes at this time. You simply tell the truth. Saying yes when you need to say no is not self-love. Saying no when you need to say no, is. It's not always easy but it's going to be necessary if you want any peace in your life. If the person you said no to isn't happy about it, that's really their problem, not yours. Everyone has a right to say no. That goes both ways.

We actually can't reasonably be anywhere other than where we are right now. It's great to hold aspirations to better yourself, or do more for the world, but just remember that these things may well come in their own good time, and trying to force a change that isn't ready to come is like trying to pop a spot with no head on it; it just gets buried deeper and makes a sore spot. Life has a surprising way of suddenly bringing an issue into clear focus at a time when we find that we have the energy and mindset to push the change through to completion. If it is to be, then its time will come.

We may look at others and see their ease. I know people who have chained themselves to petrol tanks, and others who are strictly vegan. I recognise that they went through a deep inner-process of complete honesty with themselves to arrive at their ultra-committed positions. Whether you love their ethos or loathe it, you have to admire their clarity and commitment. Still, they make it look easy. I also know many others who remain wilfully disengaged from anything personally, morally, environmentally, or politically challenging. Why is it then that some do the perceived "right" thing and others don't? Different people lead different lives which steer them to their inevitable passions and perceived responsibilities in such a way that they literally cannot do anything else. Their conscience simply won't allow it, and their personalities are relatively freer of mental and emotional obstacles to manifesting that particular destiny. We must remember that as much as we may not be able to do their job, they equally, might struggle with ours.

I remind myself of this when I think I "should" be out in the streets demonstrating against injustice. There certainly are causes that would motivate me to do this but I'm not by nature a "demonstrator" type. I'm a healer, a therapist, and a teacher. That's how I do my social work. If I was meant to be there protesting, I would be. I would not be able to do anything else. I would be compelled. I'm just not though, and that is okay. **I give myself permission** for this to be okay with me. Others are compelled to protest as I am compelled to write and teach. That's their place. I have mine, and you have yours.

There are forces and histories involved in every person's story which bring us to where we are today. As you change, through multiple experiences and learnings, so will your outlook and morality. You can force it if you wish but that's swimming against the tide, and I say the smart money is on the Zen way. Maybe one day I will hold a placard too? Maybe not. I know that if we have our hearts in the right place, then everything else will eventually follow as it must, if it is to be, in its own time.

Self-love involves bringing all of this understanding together so that there is forgiveness for our flaws and weaknesses. All is not as it seems. It's far too simplistic to compare ourselves to others and decide that we must be bad because we're not doing what they're doing. When assessing our standard of morality, it's smart to recognise that it exists within the context of what we are actually **able** to do, not just physically and mentally, but also emotionally and energetically. These are the real obstacles. Woundedness, depression, anxiety, exhaustion, stress, low self-worth (ironically), ill-health, confusion, fear, you name it. It all has an effect, and it may be impossible to overcome at this particular moment in time. Being unable or unwilling to be completely in line with your best moral compass at all times is not hypocrisy. It's life. When all of this is considered, I hope that you will arrive at the conclusion that nobody has a right to judge you harshly, and that is the reason why you should not allow anyone else to decide for you whether your heart is in the right place or not, **especially not the inner critic.**

Some people possess amazing inherent strength. Those lucky people may find it difficult to comprehend why others can't seemingly just "get it together". It's not that folks are weak or lacking morality. It's that the inherently strong are fortunate. Perhaps they escaped the wounding? Maybe their upbringing gave them everything they needed? Maybe they just have good genes? I have known what it is to look at others in my moments of strength and wonder why they are so disorganised, and I also have been on the receiving end of such disapproval in my own moments of fragility and turmoil. It's not until we have suffered deeply that we can understand both perspectives. Those who judge easily probably haven't suffered deeply.

Suffering is the great leveller.

Be patient with yourself. You may yet achieve great things but if you're berating yourself today for what you haven't done **yet**, you're going to make it a lot harder to feel the love and find the energy required to be the best person you can be. Maybe being kinder to yourself is the real sacrifice?

The inner critic will never understand this. It is comprised of the voices of those who have never experienced your pain, and that is exactly why you should completely disregard anything that he/she/it has to say!

Treat others as you wish to be treated, harm as little as possible, and recognise that the rest of it is what it is. It's outside of your control. Respect your limitations and keep in mind that your best is not a fixed quantity. It's what you've got available in any given day, week, month, or year. In other words: cut yourself a bit of slack. Life is difficult enough already.

Chapter Eight - Understanding Hatred

It is said that being treated indifferently by someone you care for is worse than having them hate you. There's truth in this. Hatred can be an incredibly powerful emotion but it is not without reason.

An interesting thing happens when you investigate the feeling of hatred. What you almost always find behind hatred is pain or fear. In order to experience true hatred, it's usually because the object of your hatred actually really matters to you. We don't experience strong emotion about things we don't care too much about.

I spoke in my book, Anger Management, about the principles of the Yin-Yang symbol. The notion is that opposing forces each contain a small component of their opposite. When a force becomes too full, it can suddenly flip and become its opposite. I used the analogy of Judo, a fighting system which takes the force of an attack and destabilises it so that the attacker over-extends and ends up on the floor. The aggressive force is now passive and defensive. It has become its opposite. Love and hate can operate along similar lines.

We can go from loving someone deeply to feeling intense hatred towards them in an instant if they betray us. Equally, we can go from hating someone intensely to loving them deeply again if a truly healing interaction takes place. Hatred is really a defence mechanism which says, "Get away from me. Do not come into my space. I am vulnerable to you. I will destroy you before I let you hurt me again." It carries this message with violent force. Hatred is a razor-wire wall fitted with loaded cannons.

When there is a truly sufficient healing experience which allows us to know for sure that we will not be (knowingly) hurt again by that person or situation, then hatred has no reason to continue to be. When the wall of hatred dissolves, it is usual to experience a great outpouring of love and relief as the dam releases its contents, that being all of the love which has been held back during the period of estrangement.

All heartbreak creates some measure of hatred, and all healing dissolves it.

This is a deliberately short chapter. Here's the take away for you: -

Understand that hatred is the flip side of love when it comes to people you are in relationship with. If you are suffering with self-hatred, it is precisely **because** you actually love yourself deeply, even though that may sound like an absurdity right now.

The hatred exists because you have been hurt, and it only hurts so much because you care so much. The hatred is keeping you separated from yourself but this is not a permanent arrangement. It is what it is right now. It may seem that bridging that gap is impossible? It may look like a chasm the size of the Grand Canyon? Please know that it's not what it seems.

I will be presenting some tools and techniques later in the book which will provide an opportunity for you to heal the source of your distress. You can become a friend to yourself again. Emotions are emotions. They are not facts. Becoming a friend to yourself is almost certainly much closer than you think. How do I know this? **Because** you care!

Chapter Nine - Failure And Success

We like to think that we are where we are as a result of our own efforts. In most respects this is true. Clearly, you can look back and see a long line of cause and effect which has brought you to exactly where you are today - for better or worse I might add.

Some of the decisions that you have made, were pored over with great care and skill, and then executed with all of the existential force you could muster. As they say, luck is the residue of design. We generally don't get much back unless we put something in. Hard work pays off. Nobody can take that away from us, and we are rightly proud of what we achieve. None of our success though comes without a fair share of failure first.

Failure is part of the process of success.

Don't skim that statement. Just think about that for a moment. They are not two opposing outcomes. They are part of a single timeline. Failure literally teaches us how to succeed.

A sense of failure is one of the greatest enemies of self-love so we're going to need some leverage on this one if we are to start valuing ourselves properly.

Let's begin with the statement:

There is no such thing as failure. There is only feedback.

It's a bit of a therapeutic cliché but it's absolutely true. I'll spare you the long list of predictable positive motivational quotes from the success gurus but let's just say that every failure is worth celebrating because it teaches you what doesn't work. It's only a failure if you let that be the end of it, and even that is not necessarily a failure. It's worth noting that some failures teach you that your chosen path isn't meant to be, or isn't what you really want. Sometimes, we might begin a project, invest resources into it, and ultimately abandon it. That's okay. That's still feedback. Your project may not succeed but you will undoubtedly have learned a lot along the way. Nothing is wasted. I've done plenty of those in my life. Changing direction is allowed.

Low self-esteem or low self-worth can be paralysing when it comes to building something of value in the world because if you are already feeling vulnerable to criticism, then it follows naturally that "failure" is the last thing you're going to be willing to risk, and all great endeavours are likely to include some failures along the way. The limiting subconscious logic is that it's better then to simply not try because if you don't try then you can't fail, right? Thus, we find ourselves impotent or paralysed.

Black and white thinking is rarely helpful generally but the pass or fail dichotomy is the worst of all offenders. I deliberately used the flashy word, "dichotomy", because it describes this situation perfectly. "Dichotomy" is defined as something which **seems** to have contradictory qualities. That's the mistake. When speaking of life-goal achievements, pass and fail are not contradictory, they are part of a process together. Okay, an academic examination may be a pass or fail scenario but most endeavours are an ongoing process. Success is achieved through a series of passes and fails, or trial and error, as we often say.

One really helpful way to tackle this problem of fear of failure is to embrace the word "**experiment**". If you approach your projects in life as experiments, then you remove the fear of failure, because you can't fail an experiment. By definition, an experiment only asks, "what happens when I do this?" It doesn't imply a judgement at the end of the process. Then, we can take what we've learned, and improve on it. Or we can change direction. Either way. It doesn't need to say anything damaging about you.

Whatever business you're in, once you start speaking to others in your field, you quickly learn that everyone "fails" along the way, and it's helpful to remember that many others have failed spectacularly before finally nailing it. While I am in favour of encouraging people to work on their wounding generally, this is one area which is likely to be difficult whether we are wounded or not. At some level, taking on a challenge is an act of courage under any circumstances. It's a bit like waiting for Mr Right instead of Mr Right Now. You'll be waiting a long time if you're waiting for the perfect conditions. Approaching your endeavours as an experiment is really the only way to go because we have to get a foot in the door somewhere. Obviously, be respectful of your limitations. Don't try to do too much too quickly. That's an invitation to overload. But, do recognise that fear of failure is based on bogus assumptions that a lack of success is a failure. It's not. It's part of the process of success. It means you just haven't succeeded **yet**.

Many business-people will tell you that the business they end up with is not the business they started. Life is no different. If we remain disengaged, **nothing** happens. Something is better than nothing. You volunteer at a local charity shop. Mr Green stops by the shop and invites you to a council meeting where you are asked to get involved with a community project, and before you know it, you're leading a team of archaeologists into the Peruvian jungle! Life does stuff like this.

I've said this before in a different context but it applies here too: -

You say "I'll do it when I feel better." I'm suggesting that "You'll feel better when you do it".

You've heard it before I'm sure but it's worth repeating. At the end of our lives, we won't regret what we did do nearly as much as we'll regret what we didn't do. Courage is not the absence of fear. It's doing what you want or need to do in spite of fear.

You are going to fail. We all are. The only difference between you and the people who succeed is in the definition of failure. See it as an inevitable part of success or feedback and you'll have far less to worry about. At some point, something good will happen.

Chapter Ten – Judgement

How does it feel to be harshly judged? It's not nice is it? If we know that it feels bad, doesn't it make sense to work towards creating a world where we all do less of it? Maybe we have to lead by example?

Feeling not good enough has been a prevalent cause of anxiety for many of my clients. Unsurprisingly, such clients usually hold themselves to exceedingly high standards. I ask them, "Do you judge other people harshly too?" I have been surprised how many of them have said "Yes."

> **If we walk around judging people all day, it's going to be pretty difficult to believe that they're not doing the same to us.**

Undoubtedly there are plenty of people who do, but that's not really any of our business. You see, the way I see it, feeling threatened by overly-judgemental people, is a failure to recognise who the problem belongs to. If someone decides to make uneducated judgements about you, how is that **your** problem? Why do **you** have to do something to fix that?

Let's look at this objectively for a moment. Think of your favourite entertainment product in the world. It could be an album, a movie, a game, a theatre production, whatever. Now go and read some public reviews. What you love, some people hate. Some will complain that it is too long, while others will say that it's too short. Some will say that it is beautiful and moving. Others will call it corny and cheesy. Beauty really is in the eye of the beholder, and none of us can be all things to all people at all times. People project their own internal feelings onto the objects which exist in the external world, and that includes other people.

In Christianity, Jesus is recognized for his goodness and purity. Still, he managed to upset some people and got crucified for it. Martin Luther-King, John Lennon, Abraham Lincoln, JFK, and Mahatma Ghandi, to name only a few modern figures, espoused the purest of intentions. They also ended up assassinated. Apparently, you can't please everyone.

If someone judges you harshly or unfairly, that really says a lot more about them than it does about you. They are seeing only through their own personal subjective filters. Those filters are often hateful and wounded. Such judgement is not considered. It doesn't ask about your genetics or upbringing, or contemplate your traumas or personal history. Harsh judgement is just anger projected onto the nearest available object. Sometimes, that's you. It's a mistake to give those opinions any credence, or feel hateful towards the people who dish this stuff out. Jesus said it right, "Father, forgive them; for they do not know what they are doing."

With a different perspective, the correct response is to feel some empathy for those who spend their lives judging everything. We can deduce that they must live in a world of negativity where they see only the worst in life. It's highly likely that they live in a state of anxiety about being judged themselves, and they are undoubtedly carrying some hidden and unresolved pain. Happy people are too busy enjoying life to spend their time pouring scorn on others. In fact, they usually derive great pleasure from lifting others up.

When you are comfortable in your own skin, it really doesn't matter what other people think about you.

If you're living in a state of anxiety about being judged then, let's begin within some recognition that part of your agenda should include being less judgemental about others. This book is ultimately focussed on helping you to judge yourself less but I'm sure you can see the logic in reducing your tendency towards harsh judgement when it comes to the world and other people, as a means to achieving that?

You might wonder how this can be achieved?

We can definitely begin the process by simply **choosing** to be less judgemental. That means recognising that you have come to an automatic conclusion about something, and then challenging that assumption with some deeper questions before it has a chance to become a position that you feel that you need to defend. It's not easy though because judgement is an unconscious process, and it is a form of emotional protection.

We need to have some understanding of why our judgements exist, and why they may be inaccurate and untrustworthy, if we are to be willing to give some of them up. They will not go easily.

Let's explore this. Be prepared to be lightly challenged now. This is not easy medicine to swallow.

My brain still throws up judgements from my formative years in the seventies, a time where the term "politically correct" meant that a politician passed an exam. These are thoughts which not even the tiniest part of me agrees with in any way but they're still present occasionally. I have to take those thoughts down as they appear. That's just part of having a brain conditioned by an environment. It's the same as dealing with automatic negative thinking. We can't necessarily do anything about the fact that a negative thought appears but we can choose not to endorse it as if it were true. It's really just the whirring machinery of the conditioned brain doing its thing. Nothing more. If we don't know this though, we can mistake these thoughts as our own.

I have an enduring memory from my school days. It was a moment of illumination for me but I wouldn't mind betting that the other thirty kids in my class have forgotten it. A teacher explained the word "prejudice" to us. Prejudice is the act of pre-judging. It is an involuntary and automatic response to a given person or situation which occurs before we have any evidence that what we think or feel is appropriate to the current situation. I pondered on this a great deal. I questioned myself. How often do I do this? The answer: A lot.

It's not surprising. Let's remember that the unconscious mind is tasked with making day to day life run on auto-pilot. Once you have learned to read, write, eat, walk, drive, talk, and type, you really never think about it again. You just do it. There's so much to learn in this world that it's super-easy for our brains to take a rain check on fully investigating anything which isn't truly important to us. Still, we have to know a little about everything, right? Or else we won't know what people are talking about and we'll be left out, or people will think we're ignorant. So, we form **opinions.**

> "Civilization advances by extending the number of operations we can perform without thinking about them." – Alfred North Whitehead

Opinions are rarely well-considered or based on thorough understanding. We gather many of our opinions from snippets of information, in a state of urgency. These include media headlines, social media articles, personal anecdotes, formal education, advertisements, parents and peer groups. As we are all learning, in this new information age, data is easily distorted, headlines can be "spun", and everybody has an agenda to protect. Lies are not called lies anymore. Now they're apparently called "alternative facts". It's extremely difficult to be sure therefore that our opinions are accurate.

That's not because we're stupid. It's because there is too much going on at any given time, for us to be able to allocate a huge amount of our limited time and energy to understanding **every** subject thoroughly. Plus, there's an awful lot of misinformation around. Even with the best intentions, it's difficult to be sure that we haven't been manipulated into going along with an agenda which has darker motivations than our own. Even the good-hearted can be led by their emotions into sinister territory.

This means that most of us end up knowing a little about a lot, and maybe specialising in one or two areas which have ignited a passion within us. We'll talk all day on our favourite subjects, and we'll listen too. We're even happy to defer to a fellow expert's wisdom if the shared passion is non-contentious. A meeting of agreeable minds is most welcome.

We're a little less welcoming though when it comes to the things that we know only a little about. Think about this for a moment. We are more judgemental toward the things that we don't really understand. We find the unfamiliar threatening and tend to take an automatic dislike to it. In the extreme form we call this reaction xenophobia (*pronounced* zen-o-phobia), which means "fear of the alien" or "fear of the other".

As irrational as this position is, there is a reason that it happens. It has evolutionary roots. Fear of anything "different" is an evolutionary response to threat from the outside world. Remember, humans lived for a long time in small, inward-looking groups. It's difficult to know for sure how early humans treated each other but it's reasonable to suppose that groups of strangers haven't always greeted each other with open arms. The "other" is a potential threat. The "other" may want to harm us or steal our resources. The "other" may bring disease. We don't know what their values or intentions may be, and the brain supplies us with feelings of hostility towards outsiders. Evolution has always erred on the side of caution. Once again, we are at the mercy of our primate programming. Unfortunately, not everybody understands this and these primal instincts can be mistaken for our own personal opinions.

We also need to remember that there is strength in numbers. Who wants to line up with the losing team? Peer pressure is extremely powerful in this regard. We will follow the majority crowd, even if that means going against our own moral code or better awareness. Attaining social reward and avoiding social punishment is high on our emotional agenda. That's another reason why we don't make a habit of questioning our opinions too deeply. Depending on your environment, to do so may result in you finding disagreement with your group, and ultimately becoming the judged yourself, if your conscience refuses to be silent. In some countries, dissent is punishable by death to this day. The pressure to conform is powerful. Some things are better left unsaid. "Pick your battles wisely" is good counsel.

In understanding our relationship to judgement then, it pays to recognise that many of our opinions are not ultimately our own. They are products of our environment, some of which we accept under duress because swimming against the tide is asking for trouble. Still, once we have them, we do make them our own and we often stand proudly behind them, even when they are logically indefensible. That's a default position because certainty is safe, and uncertainty is considered weak.

Consider then, that taking the judgements that your local culture encourages you to hold and actively pinning them on the people around you is a pretty messed up thing to do. It means that someone told you to hate someone and you said "okay". You're better than that. We're better than that.

The problem is that opinions require a justification. Once we "believe" in our position on something we simply stop noticing, or even actively avoid, contradictory viewpoints. We look only for the evidence which supports our own existing beliefs. This is known as **confirmation bias**. To every story there are two sides and a thousand shades of grey in between. That's too much to process for most people, so we pick a side and stick to it, creating ever more elaborate explanations of why we're right and they are wrong. We will potentially turn ourselves inside out, distort facts, lie, cheat, rob, or steal to reinforce our position. Heck, some people will even kill to be right. Then we end up with crazed ideologies. History is rife with such examples.

The truth is, we don't know enough to have an accurate opinion about a lot of what we hold dear. Our justifications are often drawn from headlines and conditioning rather than deep investigation. This is how judgements form and proliferate in our lives. A momentary connection with a particular subject creates a feeling, and from that point forwards we just "know" how we feel about something. We are either for it or against it. Initially, we may not even be aware of why we don't like something, we just don't, and we often have a particular aversion to anything novel. We don't like change much, so new arrivals, whatever they may be, are usually unwelcome. It's why your dad takes an instant dislike to your boyfriend, and it's why the older generation are always convinced that the youngsters of today are out of control. We forget that our parents' generation felt the same way about us. We like what we're used to. Opinions are not always backed by evidence or reason. Feelings are often the only justification we need to embrace an opinion.

So, this is what we're up against. We have other people telling us what we should like and what we shouldn't. We have a monkey brain which doesn't like change. We are highly territorial. Deep thought is hard work and potentially hazardous to our position in the group, and psychology dictates that we don't like being told what to do, so when we're challenged by opposing views, we tend to cling to our position more tightly. Letting go of all that sounds like hard work doesn't it? So…

Tell me again then why I might want to choose to be less judgemental?

There's a simple answer. Harsh judgement creates hatred, and hatred is painful. It also doesn't achieve much except to make everyone involved miserable, and that includes the person who is doing the judging. Does it really make us feel good to make others seem bad? Lately, it's become a sport. Harsh judgement is not improving our world.

Taking a morally superior position (judging) may be a strategy by which a person (or even a nation) can avoid feeling worthless themselves but ultimately it delivers only a booby prize. You've obtained your measure of comfort at someone else's cost. At some level that weighs on you. More importantly, it's going to be very difficult to judge **yourself** less harshly if harsh judgement is your default position in life generally.

I'll tell you straight out how to disarm harsh judgement in a millisecond. Ready?

Just say..."I don't know".

Saying "I don't know" does not make you stupid. It actually implies intelligence. It's okay to not know. You don't have to have strong opinions about everything. Your value is not to be measured by what you know. Let go of your need to have a strong opinion about everything and you'll learn that being judgement-free is one of life's greatest pleasures. Not having an opinion is extremely liberating.

None of us have lived another's life. Our job is to take care of our own life, not everyone else's. When you feel a snap judgement coming on, take a step back...try "I don't know" because that is the truth. You don't. Admitting that is not a weakness or a failure. You'll be pleasantly surprised by the "soft" power of not having to know everything, or even have an opinion. Neutrality is just as valid as for or against.

There is one final observation here too. We can fall into the trap of thinking that we're being judged when we're not. If you are a person who walks around judging people all day long, then as I've explained, feeling judged will be a natural consequence of that position. Some people though, judge others very little, and still walk around feeling like they stick out like a sore thumb. If you're one of them, you really need to know that your brain is screwing you over on this. Why is it one rule for everyone else and a different one for you?

The reality is that most people are self-focussed, and if their mind is on anything, it's on how **they** are being perceived, not how you are. We are self-centric. How could you not be? **You** are living your life. As far as your friends are concerned, they will love you for who you are, not who you think you should be - unless they are utterly shallow, in which case you need better friends.

"When you're twenty, you care what everyone thinks. When you're forty, you stop caring what everyone thinks. When you're sixty, you realize no one was ever thinking about you in the first place." - *Winston Churchill*

Do please try to remember that generally people don't care what you wear, how much money you have, how clever you are, what your work status is, or even how often you make mistakes. They care that you're happy, and that you treat them well.

Chapter Eleven - A Rising Tide Lifts All Boats

Setting yourself free from the awful weight of constant judgement is not the only reason to work on healing yourself and lightening up on the world. There's a secret super-bonus prize. I touched on it in the last chapter. When we are free from our own bitterness, we can derive extraordinary pleasure from holding out a hand to others. In my own healing journey, I experienced this as an unexpected consequence of doing some tough inner-work. The great beauty of this gift was that it was a genuine surprise which gave me a lot more than I had ever dared to hope for.

My goal was initially selfish. It was to somehow stop feeling utterly miserable myself. At that time in my history, I didn't recognise that so much of my misery was down to the fact that I was carrying a self-punishment agenda. Consciously, I was still blaming life. As I explained earlier, I was quickly led to the understanding that I was **unconsciously** beating myself to a pulp on a daily basis. In the process which followed, I made peace with my deepest self, and ultimately came to remember and fully embrace my original innocence. I learned that what I wanted most in the world...was to love and be loved. Not just by others but also by myself.

Then I had a massive realisation.

If this could happen to me, then it could happen to anybody.

You might say that my logic is flawed. You might suggest that this was a highly subjective experience. If we were speaking on a different matter, I would probably agree with you but this was different...**is** different. The experience of remembering what you are truly made of is basically a transpersonal one. If transpersonal is a flashy word, it means *"experiences in which the sense of identity or self extends beyond (trans) the individual or personal to encompass wider aspects of humankind, life, psyche or cosmos"* - Wikipedia.

I realised that we are messed up because we're hurt, and we can heal too.

It is no exaggeration to say that it was a revelation which completely transformed my sense of empathy towards my fellow humans. I realised that we as a whole have a tendency to beat ourselves up, but the real illumination came from understanding that this is generally an **unconscious** process. Now it all made sense. Humans walk around in a state of denial. We don't know how to process our pain. Some of us don't even realise that we are in pain and many of us don't believe it is possible to free ourselves from it, so we never even try. Let's be honest, therapy isn't fashionable is it? Unless we're in crisis, we generally don't bother. I realised that people are, generally speaking, not bad, even if they do or say bad or stupid things. They are wounded but often they don't even know it.

People need our help, not our judgement.

Human beings try to build **around** their pain. Status, possessions, and massive egos are the order of the day. We want love. That's the truth. There's no point in denying it. That's what we are. We are creatures who need love to flourish. When it's not delivered, we'll settle for something which looks a bit like it, whether that be perfection, adoration, wealth, accolades, power, or some other "achievement". If we get it, we're still miserable. It's all ultimately empty and passing. There's no substitute for love.

The problem, is that the pursuit of these imagined fulfilments is not only a distraction but it also potentially robs us of the very thing we truly want and need if we are to escape the bind – **kindness**. Love and kindness are inextricably linked. The pursuit of money, power, and status, may involve being ruthless. If that's the goal, then kindness may be snubbed, not because it's inherently impossible to be successful and kind but because it's easier to achieve those goals if you're prepared to be ruthless, and you can't be both. Those who haven't yet woken up to the fact that these pursuits won't ultimately deliver satisfaction will as yet have no concept of the dangers of sacrificing their kindness to avarice.

Like judgement, if you're not kind to others, it's going to be pretty difficult to believe that you can be kind to yourself. Scathing "opinions" about kindness will be based around the notion that kindness is weakness, or that kind people are always taken advantage of. It's a dog eat dog world they'll say. There will be a justification somewhere. We might buy ourselves a big shiny new car and call that self-kindness but the deepest self really doesn't care about any of that stuff if it's not accompanied by an inner-relationship that's worth having. Any kid with rich, emotionally unavailable parents, will tell you this.

If we are in this bind, the secret we won't reveal to ourselves, because it's too painful to hope for when our experience has been anything but, is that we'd trade it all - the wealth, the possessions, the persona, the power, all of it, for a little kindness. To be truly loved. To be a little boy or girl in the embrace of someone who would die for us. That is the ultimate safety. In some strange way, the healed human heart is not only personal. It is one which we all share, and it is a radiant jewel which waits for us all patiently to come home.

There are two types of people in the world. Those who know this, and those who don't. This is the dividing line between people who work to make the world a better place for everyone, and those who work to make it a better place only for themselves, often at the cost of everyone else.

At the risk of coming across as patronizing or superior, it's this understanding which has fuelled my passion to look past a person's presentation, to the person they are waiting to become. I get that this sounds self-important, and possibly arrogant but my position is neither. It's simply that I've tried hate. It works for a while but ultimately it hurts. I've also been incredibly fortunate to experience moments of sweetness which have left me in absolutely no doubt that the greatest prize in the world is love and kindness. It feels amazing to receive and just a delight to give. Who wouldn't want that?

Healing is universally desired at the deepest level but it's often something you didn't know you wanted, needed actually, until you get it. That's not a superior position. It's an informed one.

When people are being unkind, it's a pretty safe bet that they haven't had a taste of this yet because sweetness is a no-brainer. We can walk around angry, bitter, and judgemental, or we can see the best in things. I imagine most people would choose the latter if they knew they had an option.

The double-extra-whipped-cream-cherries-on-top-fizzy-tastic bonus is that if the majority of people did know this, and practiced it, we'd live in a much nicer world. It's not us and them. It's us and us. Only half of us know this presently, and the other half still thinks there's an enemy.

When you heal your own bitterness, you realise that some of the people around you do what they do because they haven't yet tasted sweetness. Then, instead of harsh judgement, you feel compassion for them. This is not pity. Pity is condescending. It's more like an understanding that they are acting from a place of pain, even if they don't recognise that themselves. It may be unacknowledged pain. They might shoot you, the messenger, if you tried to point it out to them, but once you have been through the process of moving through your own pain and back into love, you come to have an understanding which transcends the debate. They might not know it but you do, not because you're clever or superior but simply because a **universal** truth has been revealed to you. Hate hurts and love heals. Knowing this doesn't make us "better" than anyone else. It just means that we have an understanding which allows us to minimise the pain inside ourselves, judge less, and spread a little more love in the world because now we understand why it's worth doing.

Then, our job is to hold the space quietly and patiently until each person is ready to do their own work.

What that means in practice is continuing to **be** kindness in a world of anxiety and ruthlessness. If or when someone asks you for your help, then give it. In the meantime, just go about your business with kindness. Your presence, and all of those who join you in your refusal to be a hater, is the tide which will then lift all boats.

Chapter Twelve – We Don't Know Enough

Now, strap in because we're going to pull back from the personal perspective for a moment and take a look at a much bigger picture. I'm throwing a little curve ball in here but it's not without reason. We'll be going far out before coming right back down to Earth in the next chapter. This chapter is for people who fret about the state of the world, and the direction of Humanity.

Much as we may be unduly hard on ourselves personally at times, we are also deeply affected by the direction that we are travelling in **collectively**. We may not be fully conscious of this fact. You may have an internal narrative which doesn't dwell too much on what's going on in the world but the constant stream of bad news and negative programming which trickles into our consciousness has a negative effect at a **subconscious level** on our sense of worth. If the world is going to hell in a handbasket, as our media and influencers subliminally suggest, then we must be bad, right? What if Humanity really is nothing more than a virus with legs? Our current trajectory makes that an easy conclusion.

How can any of us have self-worth if we are convinced that Humanity as a whole is an evil, warmongering, foolish menace to itself and existence?

Nobody can deny that Humanity has done some pretty messed up things at times, and continues to do so but that's only half the story. In fact, it's far less than half. It's not all bad news.

Hans Rosling released a book recently called *Factfulness: Ten Reasons We're Wrong About The World – And Why Things Are Better Than You Think*. The book provides fact-checked evidence which illustrates that we're being sold a biased and negatively distorted perspective on the progress of solutions to many world problems. In the most important areas of human development we're doing reasonably well, and things are improving. Only this morning, I rode a biogas bus which runs on gas fuel manufactured from organic waste, producing approximately eighty percent less harmful emissions. This is great news. Clearly there are still major world issues which require urgent attention, and some areas of need and development are still worsening but generally things are getting better.

I want to share some positive thoughts and perspectives which have helped me personally to relax a bit about the state of Humanity and the world.

First of all, life! Where's the instruction manual? The closest thing we have to a collective instruction manual are the holy books. If you are a person of faith, these might soothe your existential uncertainties but they offer little explanation on how to go about solving current world problems. Whatever our personal, philosophical, or religious beliefs are, it still seems sensible to do what we can with what we can see in front of us.

It does **appear** that our physical universe began with a big bang, since the Universe demonstrably continues to expand in all directions. Then, sun-orbiting planets formed from space dust, and life appeared and evolved on Planet Earth. Most scientifically oriented people should have no reason to doubt this. The "proof" is all around us in geology. Volcanoes are still erupting today and making new land. There is no **evidenced** reason to doubt that the physical universe really did evolve as science suggests. This means that as far as we know, we're on a planet with limited space and limited resources, and what we make of this opportunity is entirely up to us. As far as we can tell, there is no definitive intervention from any outside agencies. This isn't a denial of God. It's just a "start with what you can see" position. We appear to be free to do as we see fit and then to reap what we sow – a blessing and a curse all at once. Our beliefs have no effect whatsoever on this fact. All actions really happen. Our toothaches are for real, and you can't unscramble eggs. If we screw this up, we will live or die with the consequences. If there is a God, he/she/it seems to have given us freewill.

Sanity would require then, that we engage with ourselves and the planet at the level which is apparent to us. For the avoidance of any doubt, I am fully in favour of this. That means putting aside any fantasies that someone, or something, is going to miraculously rescue us, or come along and clean our mess up for us. If that was the way things worked here, Hiroshima, Chernobyl, and Fukushima would never have happened. I suppose a miracle could happen but that's like betting your house in a poker game. There can be no excuses for wilfully trashing the planet or being awful to ourselves or the rest of life. Clearly, we have work to do here, and fast. What I am about to discuss, is in no way a suggestion then, that we abdicate our personal and collective responsibility in any way.

I am deeply saddened by how we have collectively debased ourselves and the planet we live on but in the same way that I work to see beyond the wounding of an individual to their original innocence, I also see the unwounded soul of Humanity as a truly spectacular expression of life with almost infinite potential. When we are at our best, we are astoundingly beautiful.

Unfortunately, Humanity is wounded, and therefore hampered by obstructive psychological forces. We are prone to bouts of destructive unconsciousness, and I suspect that we are powerfully influenced by at least two significant factors we should consider before judging ourselves too harshly.

The first of these, I propose, is that we are collectively traumatised. Humanity's journey across time has not been easy. How much heartbreak and hardship has been endured? Incurable disease, untreatable pain, mental illness, famine, drought, poisoning, war, torture, scarcity, earthquakes, ice ages. Contemplating the minutes, hours, and days of mental and physical suffering that people have endured throughout the ages is almost unthinkable.

In terms of deep history, human life expectancy has been somewhere between twenty to forty years of age. All of that agony and loss lives in our genetic memory in some way, and it makes us greedy and fearful. More recently, in the year 1900 the average world life expectancy was just thirty-one years of age.

World War One (1914-1918) left fifty million people wounded or dead. Twenty-three years later, we had another world war. There, we lost an estimated eighty million people. That's within the lifetimes of people many of us will have known personally. Just take a moment to soak that up. It's been rough. Many of the wounded from those wars came home, completely traumatised, and went on to conceive and parent your parents, grandparents, and great grandparents. Who knows what those horrors did to their ability to give and receive love? The pain of being forced to slaughter their fellow men, whatever flag they flew, broke many. I contend that those memories live in our genes to this day, and exert a powerful but unseen influence on our well-being.

Speaking for myself, I can feel a sadness and horror in my being, on occasion, which suggests a source far beyond my personal history. I was at Glastonbury festival one year, and I stumbled across an area called the Peace Dome. Inside the Peace Dome was the Hiroshima Peace Flame which is a flame which was lit from the embers of the Hiroshima Atomic Bomb in 1945. This flame has been kept burning ever since and can be found to this day in the Hiroshima Peace Memorial Park. I took one look at this shrine and I just broke down sobbing. I couldn't stop crying for ages. I was genuinely shocked by my reaction. It felt inside like I heard a million people scream "No" in utter disbelief that this nightmare had really happened. Was that just empathy, or was I actually connecting with something truly universal? It certainly felt like the latter.

We're still processing that pain, and we're still processing the pain from our own lives too. Collectively, I believe, we are living with the effects of trauma. We are resilient and adaptable but we're not without weakness. Shaking that cumulative pain off is not as easy as we'd like to believe it is, so is it any wonder that we aren't always at our best? I'm no fan of making victims of ourselves but let's not completely ignore the fact that we've been dealing with some very difficult circumstances, the DNA-memories of which, reverberate in our bones.

The second proposal is that we are in the teenage years of our evolution and our behaviour is not yet **entirely** self-directed. We're simply not mature, and we haven't learned to pick up our wet towels, or understand why it's even an issue. *My sincere apologies to any teenage readers. I'm about to use you as fodder for my analogy but believe me when I say that you're awesome, you make the best music, your vision is revolutionary, your hearts are huge, I envy you slightly, and I'm sure you do pick up your towels...mostly!*

Adolescence is the strange yawning gap between childhood and adulthood where both stages of development are present simultaneously. I remember being seventeen. I remember being alive in a way that was far more exciting and passionate than my experience is today. It was the heady mix of having the freedom of an adult coupled with the excitability of a child. I could see and feel things then that the adults around me couldn't. I miss those times, and many of those magical feelings are merely echoes today.

In hindsight though, I recognise that for all of the wonder of those poignant days, I was quite blinkered, and rather reckless. I also recognise that I was tragically blind to the effects my life choices had upon other people. I'm very clear about this. I didn't have poor intentions. I believe I was literally incapable of putting myself fully into the shoes of others, and as a result I was self-centred despite being well-meaning. Without wishing to be unkind to teenagers, generally speaking, that's a thing. Though contentious as a fact of science, there has been suggestion that teenage brains are less risk averse because the frontal cortex is not yet fully developed. Regardless, the only remedy it seems, is age. The brain and personality continue to mature well into our twenties and beyond. One day, we look back and ask ourselves how on earth we lived like that?

Teenagers are sensation-seeking beings with a heightened attraction to novel experiences. It's therefore hardly surprising that they'll make more mistakes during those years because they have new found freedoms to explore the world with, but they lack experience. You need to get your fingers burned before you learn to steer clear of flames. I was a studious and inquisitive kid so I had plenty of knowledge as a young man but I lacked wisdom because wisdom comes with experience and maturity.

Are we then, as a developing species, currently full of magic and knowledge but lacking wisdom?

H G Wells said, "Civilisation is in a race between evolution and catastrophe." He was probably right. We do occasionally come perilously close to collectively ending ourselves. Usually, this is because our "leaders" do something stupid, or reject viable solutions for nefarious reasons, and in a perfect world we'd have intelligent, visionary leaders.

We definitely don't. Humanity has shown itself to be slow in responding to the planetary crises we face. We now know that our oceans are littered with plastic, our air is dangerously polluted, species and habitats are becoming extinct at an alarming rate, and the ice caps are melting fast. Some people are still without food, water, healthcare, shelter, and basic sanitation. The financial system is wobbly, politics is imploding, and corruption and greed are rampant. Wars continue unabated. Ugly ideology is everywhere. The situation is depressing, and I apologise for the reminder here but I'm getting to my point.

What parent doesn't have even the slightest touch of the horrors as they see their beautiful baby girl or boy growing out of their innocence and childhood? There's a degree of inevitability that adolescence is going to be a difficult age. Mistakes will be made. The outcome is unknown. Who will your child become as they pull away from the parental units and discover themselves in a new way? All we can do is hold on, try to steer them in the right direction (invariably the complete opposite of your suggestions – reverse psychology is a must here!), and otherwise hope for the best. They'll emerge, maybe somewhat battered, and hopefully wiser, when they are about twenty something years old...hopefully. I suspect that we are currently about nineteen years old according to this analogy. We've learned to drive, we've got our first home, and a job. We're experimenting with this and that, and we're just about sure of ourselves but we've got some mistakes to make yet. This may not be failure. This may be adolescence.

Humanity is extremely close to having the technology it needs to solve most of the problems it is faced with. The knowledge is just about there. Unfortunately, the wisdom to use it lags behind, usually because the vested interests of big money are in the way. We live in unprecedented times though. No humans have ever lived through an age of information technology such as the one we have arrived in during the last decade. Can there be any doubt that this technology, despite its obvious downsides, is supercharging our collective evolution? It is unquestionably fast-tracking our technological evolution. The big question is...what is this all leading towards?

Well, science fiction, it seems, is soon to become science fact. On December 17, 1903, the Wright brothers flew the world's first practical fixed wing aircraft. In 1939, just 36 years later, the first jet plane appeared. By 1952, passenger jets were in service. In the space of under fifty years, technology went from this: -

To this: -

And that was before modern computing and information technology.

Now, Elon Musk, the man who made his fortune with the development of Paypal, has his sights set on a Mars colony with his Space X programme. Rockets have already been successfully tested. Virgin Galactic has already built the ships to take us, as tourists, into outer space. Rocket Lab are a commercial space launch company. Jeff Bezos, of Amazon fame, has the

Blue Origin programme well underway. Governments may have reduced their space-faring ambitions but it seems that some of our elite business people also have great philanthropic vision, and the resources to realise it. They get it. We need solutions. The models they are building are sustainable because they are businesses too. There are potential economic advantages to space travel. This is all happening now, not in some hoped-for future. Alongside these developments, our astronomy experts are predicting that the Universe is teeming with planets which could be viable as habitable planets for Humans. Considering what was achieved in fifty years with aviation, if the will is there, and the finance, can there be any doubt that we'll be establishing colonies off the planet within maybe a hundred years? That's conservative. Elon Musk wants it done in ten! We'll see.

The next step is to find resources. Apparently, these are plentiful in space, with asteroids being a central focus for mining. Once that's done, Humanity can establish bases, extract and build what it needs to further its ambitions, and at some point, Humanity will leave the Earth and spread out into the Universe. This shouldn't sound like science fiction. It's inevitable. Providing we don't destroy ourselves, or become the victims of a natural catastrophe before we achieve it, and providing that the will and the finance is put forward to make it happen, then it will happen. Mainly, because it may have to. Indefinite expansion into limited terrestrial space won't work. Besides, Humanity is endowed with too adventurous a spirit to stay put forevermore.

We probably won't nail it the first time around, and there will be failures and misadventures a plenty, for sure. Solutions will be found though because humans are tenacious and inventive. There are enormous challenges but there are technologies in development right now which will meet these challenges to get us started. If not immediately, then at some point in the not too-distant future. Gravity, for instance, can be simulated by designing a living area which spins (in space) creating centrifugal force. Since humans can procreate, lifespan is not an obstacle across the vast distances. Futuristic propulsion technologies and energy storage systems are already with us and developing fast. Suffice to say that exciting things are happening, and some web research on the matter will surprise you, should you be so minded. Colonising space is closer than you might think.

In 2017 Stephen Hawking told the audience at Starmus Festival: *"Our physical resources are being drained at an alarming rate. We have given our planet the disastrous gift of climate change. Rising temperatures, reduction of the polar ice caps, deforestation, and decimation of animal species. We can be an ignorant, unthinking lot. We are running out of space, and the only places to go to are other worlds. It is time to explore other solar systems. Spreading out may be the only thing that saves us from ourselves. I am convinced that humans need to leave Earth."*

It appears that at a rough estimate there may be eight hundred trillion planets in the known universe with an estimated fifty three trillion **habitable** planets out there. We don't know for sure that there are any quite like Earth, but with these odds, it's extremely likely that there exists an abundance of potentially life-sustaining planets (and probably life) and endless opportunity for expansion. There are still some major hurdles, not least of which the mind-boggling distances we'd need to traverse, but as data emerges year on year, it seems that these distances might not be as impossible as we once thought. Once we have the technology to planet-hop, time will be no obstacle.

In November 2013, astronomers reported, based on Kepler space mission data, that there could be as many as 40 billion Earth-sized planets orbiting in the habitable zones of Sun-like stars and red dwarfs in the Milky Way, 11 billion of which may be orbiting Sun-like stars.- Wikipedia.

One exoplanet in what NASA call the "optimistic habitable zone", named Tau Ceti, is only twelve light years away. The research and engineering project, Breakthrough Starshot, have their sights set on proving the concept of viable interstellar travel by sending laser-powered light sail spacecraft to Proxima Centauri, another proposed habitable-zone planet, which is 4.37 light years away. Travelling at 15-20% the speed of light, the journey will take twenty to thirty years. If they succeed, then it's a case of scaling up until manned craft can make the journey. Who knows what may follow?

We are merely one grain of sand in a Milky-Way shaped desert containing a roughly estimated 100 billion suns. Don't get me wrong. Like I said, Earth is our Mother and if we make it to this imagined future, she should be worshipped and tended like the Goddess that she is but it's entirely possible that this messy situation we find ourselves in has been as inevitable as the lack of order in our teenagers' bedrooms; an unavoidable period of partial unconsciousness, disorder, and experimentation, often with poor outcomes. The lotus flower grows out of the mud. There are no roses without thorns.

In one or two hundred years from now, we could be a space-faring species with access to unlimited resources and in possession of technologies which actually improve the environments we interact with, rather than destroy them. Maybe we'll have stopped killing each other too? There's no question in my mind that Humanity can achieve this. The real question is whether we are going to destroy ourselves, or the planet which sustains us, before we get there?

If leaving the planet sounds like fantasy or an abdication of planetary responsibility, let's not forget that we **are** making progress on solving our energy crisis, which is the main cause of pollution on the planet. Rather shockingly, at the current rate of population growth and increase in demand, our forecasted energy needs will soon far outweigh our ability to supply. New technologies are being developed which could provide limitless energy supply with no pollution. This video, now five years old (2014), highlights the top ten potential energy solutions for the future, and is well worth a watch: -

https://www.youtube.com/watch?v=uStFvcz9Or4

Nuclear Fusion energy, which is a different technology from fission (which we currently use), sits at the number one spot as the most promising future energy supply - with good reason. The aim is to harness the boundless hydrogen-based energy which fuels the sun and the stars. Technologically, it has been extremely difficult to harness this energy because it's so powerful that it's too hot to be contained but these obstacles are being overcome by the use of powerful magnetic fields which act as non-physical containers for the heat. At the time of writing, the ITER Project is well underway https://www.iter.org/. Thirty-five countries are involved in building the world's first full-scale fusion reactor, in an epic project spanning thirty-five years. It is looking increasingly likely that it will be a success, and the first plasma production is scheduled for 2025. The ITER project is not quite the end game. It is experimental, and only a bridge to full scale commercial Fusion Energy but if the technology succeeds, and is rolled out to a sufficient scale, Earth will have a means to produce clean, practically limitless energy. Fossil fuels and their associated problems will become a thing of the past.

ITER is not the only player in the game either. The UK-based Tokamak Energy project ST40 is a privately funded company with the same aims. In June 2018, they announced that they had succeeded in heating and containing plasma to a temperature of fifteen million degrees. That's hotter than the sun. They are aiming for commercial-scale fusion energy by 2030. In November 2018, fusion energy hit the headlines again, with China announcing that they had achieved a temperature of over 100 million degrees, approximately seven times the temperature of the core of the sun!

In the meantime, renewable energy sources are already making huge contributions towards a cleaner world, with new developments emerging rapidly. The Spanish company Ingelia, for instance, is doing great work in turning organic waste into useable fertilizers and fuels. They have developed a system which converts organic and sewage waste into carbon-rich fuel pellets which burn similarly to coal but without the carbon-dioxide emissions. CEO, Marisa Hernández, explained that the company's current trajectory could see them diverting half a million tons of carbon from the atmosphere by 2022.

Germany is a world leader in renewable energy use. In 2015, Germany announced that they had set a new national record by generating 78% of their energy, using renewable sources, on July 25th 2015. This was unusual. They average about 30% from renewables. There's still a way to go, and these technologies may be problematic in various ways but it's all a step in the right direction.

The race between catastrophe and evolution may be a photo finish but the progress is heartening. If these options were not on the table, I really think we could safely say that we'd be doomed.

I'm not happy about the lack of stewardship Humanity has shown towards its mother planet. She is not just a means to an end to be used and abused. She is a treasure of unimaginable splendour but it seems that the march of "progress" has been as inevitable as a marble rolling to the bottom of a hill. Even if we'd had the will to stop it, progress has always been beyond the control of any one group of people, with a life all of its own. That's not to say that one or two individuals haven't made catastrophic decisions. I can think of a few who are doing so right now.

Some of what progress has done has been shameful, and some of the damage caused definitely avoidable, and sadly irreversible, but if necessity really is the mother of invention, then it's reasonable to recognize that evolution thrives on problems. To expect that such a process would ever have been neat and tidy is to miss the bigger picture. Dwindling resources, over-population, and planetary destruction, while horrific to contemplate from today's perspective, may be the very things which force Humanity to step its game up and learn how to live harmoniously with itself and the planet, as well as finding new real estate to inhabit in the long run. If we can solve our resource, pollution, and energy problems, there's still plenty of real estate on the planet which could be ethically used. There's a heck of a lot of empty land out there. It's just not all that inviting. Technology may yet see us make gardens from deserts.

We're not there yet, and it is still very much a race between education and catastrophe but if you want to be an optimist, there really is plenty to be optimistic about.

I hold no illusions that any of this will be easy or straightforward but the possibilities for technology to transform our way of life are staggering. We may see ourselves as a scourge upon the Earth, leaving a trail of destruction as we go but I am enamoured with a very different idea.

Since we are part of existence, is it not reasonable to suppose that we are actually the eyes, ears, and hands of LIFE itself? I don't say this with any sense of grandiosity. Clearly, we are not the only conscious sensory beings. Animals are alive and conscious too. Dolphins and whales have big brains and may have epic consciousness? Intelligence is partially linked to brain size. What might be going on in a whale's brain? They may well be smarter than us but they lack hands.

We humans, are the pinnacle of land-based sentience on planet Earth, and our role has been to develop nature **beyond** itself. Life has bestowed us with opposable thumbs, and brains capable of taking such action. Why should we be so quick to judge that we are doing something wrong? We have been pushing dirt into mounds and sticking things together for a long time now. We've gotten really good at it. Yes, we've made a mess in many areas but perhaps that is what happens when creatures with freewill are set loose to make stuff; a write-off, if you will. In a way, what we have built is an **extension** of nature rather than an aberration upon it. Some of it will be a mess but some of it will be astoundingly beautiful!

Who's to say then that we have not been doing the will of life itself? Maybe, life has always had this plan? If not as a minded or wilful agenda, then as an algorithm, or an inevitability? Perhaps we, and the things we do, are only doing what comes **naturally**? How could we have done anything differently? Maybe evolution does this all over the Universe? Perhaps LIFE's agenda is to use whatever planets will sustain life, to develop species which are capable of attaining mobility in the greater Universe and launch them out into the stars to populate like seeds from a dandelion head? With an estimated fifty-eight trillion habitable planets out in that blackness, this might have happened millions of times before with different species from different planets. Time is no obstacle. In a universe which is believed to be over 18 billion years old, and on a planet believed to be 4.5 billion years old, the two million years it has taken the clever apes of Earth to reach the stars is but a minute in cosmic time. Other planetary civilisations may have done it weeks ago. That's how big time is. Suns are still being born at this very moment. And, if it is a common occurrence, then no doubt, every time it happens is as messy as the last. It's only been a few hundred years or so since we started powering machines with steam. This chaotic time of pollution and unintended consequences may simply be what the birth of a space-faring, planet-stewarding species looks like. Heady stuff perhaps but why not? Seriously, why not?

And that, is why, I entitled this chapter "We don't know enough" because we don't know enough! There's no manual to tell us what we are supposed to be doing here, and no obvious management in attendance to direct us, except that which is between our own ears. It might appear that we are completely free agents, choosing on a whim to do one thing or another but our "wilful agency" may be heavily influenced by a larger organising principle which directs the bigger picture. What is it that drives us to make art for the sake of itself? Why do we explore? Why do we build and create? Why do we continually set ourselves ridiculously difficult challenges? Why are we so restless? If evolution wanted nothing more than to sit on a grassy hill and enjoy the sunsets, then surely a blob with eyes would have fitted that bill nicely?

Instead, we find ourselves with fingers and precision, drive, ambition, logic, reason, language, aesthetic awareness, dreams, visionary capacity, and of course the most important aspect of all being - love. No, Humanity is not an aberration. We are in some way a **celebration** of existence. We are one of the vehicles that life uses to be aware of itself, to explore itself, and to continue expanding and transforming itself, and this process is currently forging ahead at breakneck speed. The ongoing progress in medicine, technology, and ethical understanding is pointing us in a direction which may exceed our wildest dreams, despite those who wish to hold it back. The good news (and the bad news) is that nobody is actually wholly in control of this thing called LIFE. As my good friend likes to cryptically remind me, "This thing is bigger than both of me".

This chapter has been a long detour I know but I hope that I have challenged some of the depressive perspectives you might have picked up along the way. Grandiosity and arrogance are ugly qualities. Superiority and entitlement are even worse and humans are all too easily seduced by a sense that they "own" the world. For those of us who recognise that this is a position which lacks humility, we may be tempted to arrive at a knee-jerk conclusion that we are an ugly species which has ruined a beautiful planet. There's truth in that but I also propose that's unnecessarily negative thinking because there may be a much larger picture yet to emerge.

Yes, we need to shift away from a position of ownership to one of stewardship, and it won't be easy because there are political, financial, and psychopathic forces at work in the wounded soul of Humanity which value power and possession over equality, co-operation, and stewardship. They encourage us to do the same but let's not throw the baby out with the bathwater. Jimi Hendrix paraphrased Chinmoy when he said:-

> **"When the power of love overcomes the love of power, then the world will know peace."**

We're not there yet. The mainstream meme-makers have an agenda. They sell news, and bad news sells best. In addition to selling stuff to us, those who value riches, power, oppression, and war above freedom and compassion, also like to keep the masses in a state of **fear and scarcity**. Fearful, financially needy masses are easier to control and manipulate. "Divide and rule" is dominant presently, so that's what gets served up the most. Be aware that it's not the full picture. This stuff is not an accurate representation of what Humanity is all about, and the narrative is deliberately designed to keep us dumbed down, distracted by horror, in a state of scarcity, disempowered, and anxious. Make no mistake. I'm no conspiracy theorist but it is **deliberately** peddled. We are bad news junkies, and the dealers have us right where they want us because it brings them money and power which they equate with security. They certainly don't want us to love ourselves, or to be overly-educated about the things which really matter. We might actually start caring enough to demand change. That's not to say that co-operate, protect, and serve is not on its way but it won't happen unless we fight for it.

We don't **have to** accept their worldview. We can fight back.

The voices of doom shout the loudest, and thereby maintain the illusion of majority, but in fact, they are in the minority.

Humans are mainly a force for good. It's simply that it's much easier to destroy something than it is to build something, so those who don't recognize co-operation as a strength wield disproportionate power, and unfortunately, the ones with all the power are ironically the ones who are in a position to implement the solutions because they hold the purse strings.

The solutions are there. The will to implement them isn't because there are conflicts of interest, and political pressures. Solutions make the powerful less powerful, and the rich less rich. This may always be a problem, but thankfully, overall, we tend to do our good work despite them, and this must continue. Eventually, selfishness and cruelty will have nowhere left to hide but only if we are willing to call it out when we see it. This is a battle which is being waged every day as we speak.

We can recognize that there is immense goodness in Humanity. There is a majesty in Humanity which we have not even had an opportunity to fully recognise yet, and it is truly astounding. For those who can taste it, this understanding can be held quietly, without arrogance or superiority but with true humility. It doesn't require the approval of others. Those who know how to live with kindness and care simply get on with doing it, and thank goodness they do because without them we really would be in trouble. Many of the technologies which may save us, and our planet, are being independently produced, and we ourselves are responsible for the cultures we choose to live in. We do have some power. We have a voice. At the very least we can let it be known that we're not okay with a destructive status quo.

We can feel grateful in life rather than entitled because in some way the splendour within us is not **because** of us. We are merely the trustees, and our job is to honour it. Self-love is not only personal. It is collective too. I'm not buying what the naysayers are selling. I think we're better than that, and I recognise that we cannot step into our greatness until we believe in it. We won't believe in it until we recognize its presence, and that won't happen if we don't look for it. I hope you'll choose to find, and express, the majesty within you too? That can be as simple as a smile at a stranger, or flowers in a window-box. In some mysterious way, these things count for something. These are simple expressions of beauty, and every meaningful gesture tips the scales in favour of a better world. Everyone has something to offer. Be a builder, not a destroyer, and reject the notion of a grey world. It's what we make it. Let's make it better.

Chapter Thirteen – Culture

Okay. Coming right back down to Earth now.

Unfortunately, recognizing your (our) greatness is not always encouraged. I am extremely fortunate and grateful to live in a modern western culture which offers an amazing amount of personal freedom, choice, and security. We in the west, largely enjoy a high degree of civility, education, and autonomy. There are problems, massive problems, and we all know what they are but the stated **agenda** of western civilisation, at least at this moment in time, is to extend freedom and well-being to its people, to make life worth living. It gets a lot wrong but mostly its heart is in the right place.

As mentioned, there are ever-present dark forces gathering in opposition to this agenda. Constant attacks upon freedom and common sense are perennials. Hatred takes root in places but it is resisted, and for that we must be thankful. Most people in the west have their basic needs met, and despite the destructive greed and bitterness which sours the mix in times and places, **overall,** we as people have an ethos which values fairness, kindness, freedom, expression, and compassion. I know how sweeping this generalisation is. Much as I'd love to muse and debate on what needs improving and how we might make things better, the focus here is on self-love and emotional protection.

From a western perspective, culture is not always on your side. Modern western culture places a huge emphasis on the acquisition of wealth, status, power, and possessions, as a means to happiness. There's a central reason for this – Capitalism. Capitalism itself isn't inherently worse than any other organizational system. History shows that all economic models have their pros and cons. We're not here to debate this, so let's just acknowledge that capitalism is the model we have and use in the west. Capitalism has many advantages but one major downside to it is that it relies on encouraging us to continue buying goods and services in order to sustain itself. That means that…

Capitalism requires us to feel dissatisfied with what we have in order to do business.

You may well already be in possession of this understanding but if you've never really considered it fully, please take a moment to pause and think about that. Now, personalise it.

> **Capitalism wants <u>you</u> to feel bad about yourself, and what you (don't) have.**

Capitalism doesn't ever tell you this though. In fact, it tells you that it wants you to feel great about yourself but inherent within its message is, "You'll **only** feel great about yourself when you have what we're selling. Buy our stuff to feel better".

> **The implication of course is that if you don't have what they are selling, then you're not good enough.**

To be fair to capitalism, sometimes the "buy our stuff" message is completely trustworthy. I buy headache tablets. They work. I feel better. I can get a dose of headache pills for about six pence. Not every company is Evil Corp Inc. If all business were conducted ethically, with well-being and care for the planet being as important as profit, then capitalism itself need not be a destructive force. Many businesses are working on it. One for the future…we hope.

Nonetheless, do we really fully understand how insidious the effect of this programming is upon our sense of self-value? I'm repeating here what I've written before so I'll keep to the point. Media and capitalism shows us what "perfect" looks like, tells us that's happiness, and then asks us to be that. Most of us are wise to the game, and learned long ago that we're never going to look like Brad, or have abs like Jen, and don't get too upset when product X doesn't deliver on its promise. The lure works though. A study conducted on a group of 100 women in the UK found that British women spend £70,294 on their appearance in their lifetime, which equates to £112.65 per month, a significant proportion of most people's disposable income after bills.

Even if we are wise to it, we are still affected to some degree. I suspect that this is impossible to fully escape unless you make a hermit of yourself on a mountainside.

The goal here then, is to have an awareness of the influence that capitalism and culture has upon us, without being at the mercy of it.

There is much to enjoy. It really does make us feel good to upgrade something that's worn out, slip into new socks, buy new shoes, eat fancy food, take a luxury holiday, make home improvements, wear something sophisticated, or receive an accolade. These are some of the pleasures in life, and excepting any abuses in the supply chain, these are not bad things in and of themselves.

Culture and capitalism become problematic when there's a great big vacuum where your self-worth is supposed to be. That void can be a black hole, sucking everything around it right in. The mistake is believing that consumption and acquisition can fill that empty space. On a global scale, we end up with fortune hoarding, psychopathic power grabs, and ruthless exploitation of people and the environment for greed. On a personal level we find hoarding, addictions, and chronic dissatisfaction in evidence. If we are struggling financially, then our culture can make us feel like we have no stake in it if we're not participating in the endless acquisition of status, wealth, and brand names. The subliminal message is "If you're not buying, then you have no value".

We are not what we own, consume, or achieve, and if we fail to understand this, then our self-worth is in an extremely vulnerable place. You are the object of value. Not your possessions, consumables, or status.

A new player has entered the arena, and it's big. Actually, it's gigantic. That of course, is social media. You probably already got this memo but just in case you missed a meeting, one of the most damaging aspects of social media is the fact that what is shared publicly is not truly representative of what is happening personally. If "keeping up with the Jones's" was yesterday's obsession, then today it's all about presenting yourself and your life as absolutely fantastic on Facebook, Twitter, or Instagram. What we see on everybody else's social media pages are the highlights. If we're emotionally healthy, we'll be happy to see others having their moments of joy but we'll know that's only a slice of the real picture. If we're not feeling okay however, and we don't understand that the slog and miseries of daily existence are kept firmly out of sight from our eyes, then we can quickly conclude that everyone else is constantly happy and having a great time, leading us to feel that our lives are significantly worse than everyone else's. That translates as "My life is not good enough", and often "I'm not good enough".

We also now understand that praise, achievements, victories, problem solving, and acquisitions create chemical "feel good" rewards within the brain, in the form of serotonin and dopamine, the same chemicals people take drugs like cocaine and MDMA to stimulate. We can't get enough of the stuff, even if it's costly.

These little "thumbs up" icons have become a form of currency for acquiring these shots of feel-good medicine.

In case you don't know, this is the symbol for a Facebook "Like". When somebody sees your post, they can click the button underneath and it shows that someone "liked" your content. It all began perhaps innocently enough but now that social media is so central to many people's lives, chasing "likes" or other forms of social acknowledgement has become extremely important to many people. It's been likened to teenage crack cocaine. Conversely, the absence of "likes" or "comments" can feel like a snub by the online community. Again, the well-adjusted will think nothing of the radio silence. Those with a self-worth vulnerability though can easily assume that the silence is a signal that their input is without value. There's another dose of "I'm not good enough" right there, and it's particularly powerful among the younger members of our communities.

Social media is often shallow. Most people use it primarily as a form of entertainment. I've seen message threads which run for days because somebody posted a single four-letter word, and I've seen other posts with enormous meaning air to complete silence. Clearly, it's not brilliance which gets attention. It's entertainment value. Social media is not a bad thing, and neither are "likes" but if our sense of self-worth rests on how many people we have on our friends list, or how many people like our posts, we're once again in an extremely vulnerable position. My recommendation is that deciding what you're worth based on social media feedback should be keenly avoided!

And finally, before closing, there would be a glaring omission if I did not acknowledge the role of religion in culture. I'm acutely aware that some of my readers are of a religious persuasion and others aren't, which leaves me in a tricky position because I'm not in the business of being contentious. I'm here to help, so go easy on me please?

As far as self-love is concerned, there are some religious perspectives which are quick to minimise the importance of the self and emphasise service to God. Others say there is "no-self", and many religions include asceticism (abstinence from sensual pleasures/implementation of self-imposed suffering) as part of their practice, essentially in an effort to "devalue" the role of self and be in service to the divine.

I'm all for service. I agree that we are at our best and usually our happiest when we are helping. What I will say though, from a therapeutic perspective, is that if we engage in a lifestyle of "service" which puts so much strain on us that it makes us ill, we'll end up not being of service to anyone! I speak from experience on this. I endured ten years of severe unwellness and misery as a result of trying to do the "right" thing, ideologically. During that time, I was barely surviving. Other than just about holding down a job, I was certainly not "serving" anyone or anything in an abundant way. Self-love is an important component of wellness. If you are not loving yourself, it's going to be very difficult to love anyone/thing else fully, and I'd suggest that this is not the intention of your religious practice. In addition, it's worth saying that if you want to be in "service" to God, then the best way to do that is to be a light in the world. In other words, be happy. When you are illuminated, you are a beacon of hope and inspiration to others and you'll achieve great things. Surely, that's a logical plan?

With only a few exceptions, the majority of religions leave room for self-love in them. If your religion is making you feel bad about yourself for any reason, be aware that there may be another way to interact with your faith so that you can be kinder to yourself without sacrificing your beliefs or commitments. I'm being deliberately unspecific here. Speak to others from your faith. Find out how they manage these complexities. Do find a way though because you won't be at your best if your religion gives you reason to be down on yourself or others.

Chapter Fourteen - Body Shame

Here's a true story which might just put things into perspective for you. Mrs C and I were on holiday in Tenerife. We were strolling down the beautiful Los Christianos beachfront and we noticed a young couple who had stopped right in the middle of the busy walkway. They both had rippling muscles, great tan, silky smooth skin, and teeth which sparkled at you as you got close. She was dressed in a skimpy pink bikini, and he was wearing nothing but bulge-hugging grey sweat shorts.

As we approached, we could see that he was rubbing his chiselled stomach up and down (to accentuate his six pack) and his hand was moving just a little too close to his nether regions, with each sweep going just inside the top of his shorts. They weren't really doing anything other than just standing there looking out to sea. The obvious message was "Check out my body!" Well, you know, I **was** impressed. It must truly have been hard work to get into that shape, but after the millisecond of admiration, I was struck by an altogether different impression. It was something to do with the way he was rubbing himself (*everybody here must want to have me*) that just made me go "Yeeeurgh!"

I looked around and saw the same reaction on other faces too, women particularly, as people gave them a creepy wide berth. To say that they stuck out like a sore thumb among the 99% of "average" slightly wobbly humans in the vicinity is an understatement. My wife and I just looked at each other with a knowing look. They were being noticed but not for the reasons they probably thought they were. Yes, I get the irony on my part. That is a judgement but there is such a thing as making a spectacle of yourself. I'm afraid there was no avoiding this one.

Imagine the relentless regime of diet and exercise they must have undertaken to achieve those eye-candy physiques, only to ruin the long-coveted moment of beachfront glory with an ill-conceived display position. You know, kudos on the body and all, but the point is, look at how **flimsy** that greatness is.

Much as we might like to believe that a "perfect" body (what is that by the way?) will bring us adoration and respect, it will deliver the exact opposite if you're creepy or conceited about it. And that's before we factor in that many people are going to envy you purely because you've managed to do what they haven't, making you not adored, but a blank canvas upon which people will project their own sense of body failure. I'm not suggesting that such projection is healthy but it is a fact. A perfect body is a fragile foundation upon which to rest your self-worth. If getting one consumes your every thought and moment, then the rewards are questionable.

That's not to imply in any way that all body-conscious people are megalomaniacs, nor that we shouldn't strive to keep our bodies in the best condition possible, but it is fair to say that we can't hide our natural and human imperfections behind a sculpted body. Ironically, achieving body-perfection is just as likely to make us a target for scrutiny as it is an object of adoration. That's not what you're hoping for as you do your three thousandth sit up this week is it?

It takes a fairly extreme lifestyle to knock ourselves into that kind of shape. I've tried and failed more than a few times, exhausting and depressing myself in the process. I'll freely admit that my ego would love to look in the mirror and see a ripped Adonis staring back at me but the price tag is eye-watering, and for people built like me, who would rather chew an arm off than forego cake and do extreme sit ups for the next thirty years, unaffordable. Even if you achieve it, you've got to keep it up if you want to stay that way.

If you're super fit, this isn't a shot at you. You genuinely have my respect and admiration. For many different reasons though, including that it's just not a priority, a lot of people never achieve it, yet still suffer significant guilt and shame. This chapter is for them.

I come from a family line of fat people and I was a fat child. I have been slightly overweight for most of my entire life, excepting a short period from about thirteen when I simply didn't eat, so I'm obviously biased on this subject. Nonetheless, I only have to look around me to see that a small minority of people actually sport a "perfect" body. That figure diminishes considerably in the over-thirties.

There are countless studies on body-satisfaction levels but they all tell roughly the same story. Most of us are unhappy with our body size and shape. The University Of North Carolina School Of Medicine published a study in 2013 which showed that only 12.2% of women over fifty were satisfied with their body size, and of them, a further percentage were unhappy with one or other aspect/s of their body. In a survey of five thousand women undertaken by REAL magazine in the UK, only 3% of women said they were completely happy with their bodies and 73% said they think about their size and shape every day. Six out of ten said their body image led them to feel depressed.

The picture is not much better for those with youth on their side either. Figures vary, depending on where you draw your research from but a high percentage of young people are highly anxious about their body size and shape, with problems developing from as young as six years old. Social media platforms supply ready-made photo alteration apps that our kids routinely use to alter their photographs before they post them online. This practice has led to a crisis in real-world body-image anxiety. Having posted digitally altered images of themselves online, people are becoming increasingly anxious about being seen in the flesh, lest they be busted on their deception when they arrive looking nothing like their online images. Agoraphobia and body dysmorphia are at an all time high as a result.

This is nothing short of a dissatisfaction epidemic, and it has mental health implications far beyond simple vanity. Using figures drawn from a 2007 study by Hudson et al. following over nine thousand people, it was concluded that about twenty million females, and ten million males in the United States will have a clinically significant eating disorder during their lifetime.

The current cultural idea of body perfection isn't necessarily healthy either. Our genetics decide where our fat deposits go. If a six pack or a firm butt are your measure of success, your body may hold the last of your fat reserves in the particular area you're obsessed with shaping, which may require you to become seriously underweight to achieve the results you want. Being underweight has serious implications for health which are every bit as serious as obesity. Poor immune system function, infertility, anaemia, brittle nails/thin skin, hair loss, muscle wastage, and ultimately organ failure and death can all be the result of malnourishment. When the body has nothing to eat, it eventually eats itself, literally. If you starve your body and survive in the short-term, it can knock ten, twenty, or thirty years off your expected lifespan in later life.

When we see ultra-thin models held up as an ideal to aspire to, we are not being told about the anorexia, bulimia, laxative misuse, amphetamine abuse, and literal starvation which made that body possible. It would be unfair to suggest that all slim people are unhealthy or engaging in damaging behaviours. Some people are built slim, but if you're not naturally one of them, then trying to mimic those body shapes is likely to be bad news for you.

So just what the heck is going on here? How have we arrived in a position where the vast majority of us live with daily anxiety about how our bodies look? Well, if you listen to the messages which are broadcast into your brain from every billboard, radio, magazine, website and tv screen, it's all because you're a big fat failure. You're fat and misshapen and it's your own fault because you're a sedentary gluttonous pig with no self-control. What's wrong with you? Get a grip! Learn to restrain yourself. Do more exercise. Oh, and by the way...we've got a special on supersize meal deals this week. Buy one today!

In western culture, the assumption that we should all conform to a slim body shape has, until recently, remained enshrined as sacrosanct. Those who have dared to challenge it have been shamed, blamed, and ostracized. While it is true that obesity is a very real problem which needs confronting, we can be sure that shaming each other, or ourselves, for the most part, is not the most effective way to solve that particular problem. As we all know, food is a comforter. If we make people feel bad about themselves, they're just going to seek solace in more food.

When a person showed up at my consulting room in a state of distress, I had to figure out what needed to happen if we were to restore control and well-being. Usually, that boils down to one of two options. Either change the situation, or change the way that the situation is being perceived. As a general rule though, we focussed on helping them to reduce their stress and have a better relationship with themselves. Invariably this did more to help them get control of their weight than placing them on a diet. Sometimes however, humans are trying to fit a square peg in a round hole. Then it's my job to point out that what they are trying to achieve is not in line with realistic expectations.

Many of us have spent our lives trying to whittle ourselves down to fit in the round hole, but what if the problem isn't our peg shape but the fact that there's only one hole?

If we looked at our collective size-anxiety as a problem-solving exercise, we'd have to conclude, given the facts, that most of us don't fit into the round hole. From an engineering perspective, we probably need to make some new holes...maybe some square ones...maybe some star-shapes, maybe an octagon or a triangle here and there? The current situation is logically absurd. The line is, "This is the shape. Fit in it, or live in shame". And, we all agree to play by those rules because as usual, the majority rules. That doesn't mean it's correct. Still, we just don't seem to be able to get our heads around the fact that the problem isn't our dieting prowess or our body-shaping efforts but that the goalposts are so narrowly defined that we'd all need to be named Ronaldo to score a goal.

Humans are great at making terrible decisions en masse for reasons discussed earlier, but in addition to that, there are more sinister motivations behind the cultural movement to keep us in a state of fat-fear and starvation. Skinny sells, and the vanity industry has its tentacles in just about every conceivable facet of our lives, from what we eat, to what we wear, to how we consume, exercise, play, love, and feel. It's the greatest scam ever devised. Get people to hate themselves and then sell them a solution which will never actually deliver in the long run. Then you can sell it to them again. How do we know this? Well, research shows that approximately 95% of people who lose weight go on to regain the weight plus more. Many people don't keep it off for a year and the 95% figure relates to a five-year period. Healthy living is great, but diets, on the whole, don't work.

Is this because we are weak? No. It's because our bodies don't actually want to be ultra-skinny. We can force them to be so by denying them the calories necessary for fat storage but they don't like it. Fat is nature's energy conservation system. When you force your body to burn its fat reserves through starvation and exercise, the body takes corrective action by slowing the metabolic rate down so that it burns calories as slowly and efficiently as possible. When, at some point, your willpower finally gives out, the body, after months of starvation, will encourage you (with ravenous appetite) to eat the most calorie-rich foods available. It then gathers and stores every single calorie you consume to replenish those vital life-saving stores of energy.

Just to make sure it's prepared for the next famine it keeps that metabolic rate as low as possible. When you return to eating a "normal" (unrestricted) diet, then your body hoards those calories as fat with much greater urgency than it did before you starved it to lose weight. You're in a worse position after you diet than you were before you dieted. This is why people tend to regain more weight than they lost. The only way to sustain skinny is to live life in a state of constant hyper-vigilance about what passes your lips. Even if you're slim, you'll need to keep up the body toning if you want to retain the look. Some people may be okay with that, and a minority achieve it, but that doesn't mean that those of us who either can't or won't live like that should be consigned to the reject pile.

The dieting industry knows this full well. If it's not a conspiracy, then it definitely is a confused state of affairs. Our culture is sending us a seriously mixed message. On the one hand it's screaming at us to consume more, and on the other, it's telling us to restrict and restrain ourselves. As we can see from the current crisis in youth body-anxiety, it's had its hooks in us from such an early age that we've had no chance of dodging the bullet. The message has always been "be slim or be ugly". It's not a new phenomenon either. Corsets, the ultimate "skinny is beautiful" statement, date back to the 16th century.

If we go back to the question of whether we change the situation or change the way we perceive the situation, we find ourselves culturally in a bit of a catch 22. The culture won't change until we create a new perspective collectively but we can't create a new perspective while we continue to subscribe to the round peg ideal. Currently, there are stirrings from the side lines but there's no sign of serious cultural change. We have a whole generation of kids who are desperate to shrink or alter themselves to fit in, so we must conclude, for now at least, that the situation cannot be changed. Or at least, not immediately, and we need relief from our body shame now, not in a decade. That leaves us with the remaining option of changing how we perceive the situation. We'll need to do it for ourselves despite the messages coming across the airwaves.

If you have struggled with feelings of not being good enough because you don't like your body, the first thing I want to say to you is that you need to stop being angry with yourself and start being angry that you've been sold a lie which has caused you to feel awful about yourself for a long time. There will be readers, I know, who have literally tortured themselves on this matter, possibly for a lifetime. I've pulled a few of my own fingernails out at times. I don't do that anymore but I'd be lying if I said I'm at perfect peace with my own body-image. I'm working on it. The cultural conditioning runs extremely deep. In addition to this, we are also battling a negative bias that the brain provides. This requires constant tackling.

I'd like to share here a short blog post I wrote a while back on the issue: -

Youth and beauty are over-rated!

March 15, 2017

Morning! A man walks up to a Zen Buddhist hot dog vendor and says "Make me one with everything". Yes, I know you groaned.

The man hands over a ten-pound note. The Buddhist replies "Do you have anything smaller? I'm afraid I can't offer you any change!" Ok. I'm stopping now.

Maybe it's because I'm British, or maybe it's simply human but I've never much liked the sound of my own voice, or the sight of myself in most pictures (I am genuinely very un-photogenic though!) Over the years, I've learned to stop caring. I realised that for the most part, no-one else cares, or notices! I mean you'd have to drop at least three stones in weight before anyone says to you "Er...have you lost some weight?" It makes you wonder then why we bother to get so stressed out about our current status?

The idea that anyone (other than maybe a judgemental partner) will think any less of you because you gained ten pounds is actually ridiculous. Still, much as it would be a Zen-like miracle or wonder to experience ourselves, like our hot dog, as being one with everything, we don't. We are self-centric. You're the first person your eyes go to in a photograph, you stick out like a sore thumb, and when you hear yourself on tape with others, everyone else's voice sounds fine but yours is weird!

We need to recognise this phenomenon for what it is. You are not the funny looking person, and your voice is not weird. It's to do with your brain having a negative bias. The human brain is hardwired to look for what might be wrong. You think you look bad in that photo? Have a look back at it twenty years from now! You'll think you were Adonis or Venus herself.

Youth may be wasted on the young but that's no reason not to enjoy every part of our lives. Youth, I say, is over-rated anyway. If you think about it, you spend the first sixteen years of your life trying to be older. Then, you have a period of about ten years where you're the boss, and then it all goes downhill from there, right? I mean it's ridiculous. If those ten years are the only times you can feel good about your looks, and most youngsters don't, even then, then surely, we're missing something?

Remember. You are lovely. Your brain is doing a number on you.

Do photographs of you look like this?!
Your brain is doing a number on you.
Everyone else sees you as beautiful x

www.youcanfixyouranxiety.com

Ignore it!

Then we have the idea that once we're forty, we're "past it". You're kidding me aren't you? If I could have known twenty years ago what I know today I would have my fingers in so many pies I'd run out of fingers. My Dad's the same. At seventy something he's more passionate and engaged in life than I've ever known him to be. No, life deepens and matures with age every bit as well as a fine wine or a delicious Comté!

If you're feeling gutted that you're getting older, you are definitely barking up the wrong rosebush. Savour it. Enjoy it. Youth is a flash in the pan, and beauty is way more than skin deep! (End)

It might also interest you to learn that human beings receive a new skeleton every twelve years. Not overnight of course. The human frame changes with age – widening, shortening, distorting. Being unable to fit into your skinny jeans at forty may have less to do with your belly fat than it does with the fact that your skeleton is a different shape now. Our metabolism naturally slows with age. A thirty-year old must eat 10% fewer calories than they did when they were twenty to maintain the same body weight. In addition to a changing frame, our ears and noses are known to continue growing larger into older age as the effects of gravity do their worst.

Cosmetic surgery is now more popular than ever before. Breast augmentation tops the list as the most popular procedure, up over 57% in the last five years. The question is, are we doing it for ourselves, or are we doing it because we are in competition with others or because we don't feel good enough? There's no doubt that plastic surgery can genuinely improve people's lives but it's not without risks or costs. Grown adults making their own decisions for their own happiness is one thing, but the pressure to slice and dice our own bodies to fit in should raise some eyebrows.

Once menopause hits, the body undergoes some radical revisions as a result of shifting hormone patterns. Men don't escape either. Though less clearly clinically defined, they have their own version of menopause. It's simply illogical to expect long-term conformity to a narrowly defined definition of "good enough" when all of this is going on, and we really need to fully reject that definition of what okay means and stop perpetuating it among ourselves. We are up against it, and a little bit of fighting spirit is called for. The problem is not with our bodies. They are as nature made them. The root of our discomfort comes from the unrealistic expectations that our increasingly vanity-obsessed cultures are telling us we should make our own.

Although I've focussed mostly on weight here, the same goes for any other shade of "different" too: underweight, short, tall, freckled, ginger, black, brown, white, bald, hairy, baby-faced, or wrinkly. You name it. Human beings come in a mind-boggling variety of colours, shapes, sizes, and models, which go through continual change as they age. This could be a cause for wonder and amazement rather than disgust or aversion. Remember you have a choice in how you view this fabulous array of diversity.

So, let's get this straight.

The primary purpose of your body is as a vehicle.

You are not an inert object whose primary purpose is to be visually admired. We call that art, and sure, you can make art of your body if you wish, but if you fall for the lie that looking good is the **only** thing your body is good for, you're going to forget to use it to do what it's best at – living. Personally, I agree with the notion that your body is a temple and a nightclub. I also think there's real wisdom in the comical image of sliding into the grave all used up, carrying a Martini (if that's your thing.) Your body is there to be used. Not abused. There's a difference.

I spoke a while back with a middle-aged lady who had recently lost her husband to cancer. He had said to her that one of his biggest regrets was not spending more of his money. We put-off life for tomorrow, right? I can take the holiday when my nose looks right, or when I've lost twenty pounds. Screw that. Live now. Spend your days, don't save them. When they are gone, they're gone, and nobody knows how many they have left.

I was listening to a radio show and somebody explained that we spend our lives working all hours with the dream that one day we will retire, relax, and spend all our hard-earned gains on pleasures. The caller suggested that it might be wise to consider "taking" some of our retirement early if we get an opportunity to do so. Why wait until you're seventy to enjoy yourself? Not everybody will make it to that age, and even if you do, you may not be physically able to do what you used to be able to. It's the same with our time.

Let's celebrate the lines on our faces as evidence of a million moments expressed in a thousand experiences had. Let's think of our love-handles as evidence of a thousand joys on the lips (screw the hips) and remind ourselves that they are wonderful to snuggle up to in bed. Let's embrace the scars on our hearts as evidence that we took some risks.

Let's remember that life is too short to be spent in the pursuit of "perfection" at the cost of life's greatest pleasures.

In summary, the message is that culture is not your friend on this issue. Many of us will never be able to measure up to the weight and beauty goals of a vanity-obsessed culture, and if that means that we will consign ourselves to a lifetime of not-good-enough-ness, then that really needs to be not okay with us. We need to recognise that the fault lies with a shallow and judgemental element of our cultural establishment which relies on us being weak and needy so that they can keep us enthralled to constant dissatisfaction and buying their "improvements". This might sound radical but it's really not. What other reason do you need to explain why only 3% of women (over 50s) feel satisfied with their bodies? We are so deeply indoctrinated at this point that we almost literally cannot see what these figures tell us. It cannot be right that 97% of women are abnormal. The truth is staring us in the face. Normal is the 97%. The 3% are simply examples of **extraordinary** beauty.

We need to reject these ridiculous aspirations robustly, and decide for ourselves what beautiful is. It hardly needs saying but just in case anyone is any doubt on this, what is beautiful is kindness, and it lives on the inside. I really don't care if you've got seven arms and two heads. If you are kind to me, I will love you. If you're still figuring out how to be kind, I'll cut you some slack if you get it wrong once in a while and still love you, as long as your heart is in the right place. Most are. That's the barometer of a sane culture.

Later in the book, I'll be offering you some tools which are designed to help you come into a place of deeper acceptance and self-forgiveness, as well as explaining how to identify the roots of your difficult feelings and make peace with your past and present (without surgery!) You can certainly use those tools to work on any body-shame concerns you may be carrying. Make a mental note now and add it to the list when you get to the relevant chapters.

I don't expect that one short chapter in this book is going to touch the sides as far as tackling a lifetime of negative body-image is concerned but what I do hope is that I can at least point you in a new direction. Do a web search on "Body Positive" for a new world of support.

We know that standing up to what is essentially bullying from our culture isn't going to be easy, but as our self-worth develops it becomes much easier.

Chapter Fifteen – Other People

It has been said that people are the weirdest objects in the world. Culture may direct us collectively but what other individuals think, feel, and do, is sometimes baffling to our sensibilities. If we are to maintain a strong sense of self-worth in a world where our viewpoints so often conflict with others, we are going to need to have an understanding of why it's okay to agree to disagree with others and remain true to ourselves in the process. In addition to this, I want to briefly explore why some people may want to de-value you without good reason, and explain why their behaviour can be safely ignored. This chapter comes with a special supporting hand for those who find themselves in any "minority" group, or indeed, those who are "different" for any reason.

I was introduced to the model of "Attraction, Cohesion, And Repulsion" many years ago, and it's been a very helpful tool for me in maintaining a balanced view of the world, and my place in it. I'd like to share it with you here.

The idea is that there are three different reactions which can occur when we interact with other people, which are as follows:-

Attraction

*Attraction occurs when two people share enough similarities in their outlook and person to have a ground of being where they can comfortably meet but enough differences that the other remains intriguing. The attraction part happens **because** of their differences, not despite them. We experience mutual attraction with people when we can add mutual value to each other's lives. Energetically, the relationship may have moments of disagreement and tension but a common bond of mutual respect and interest usually continues. Attraction is recognised as an ideal condition for romantic love to develop and endure. Differences keep things interesting.*

Cohesion

Cohesion occurs when two people share many identical values, interests, and qualities. They just "get" each other, and are likely to have a very harmonious relationship and a strong bond. This relationship may lack the "spark" of attraction because of its predictable nature, but it will be dependable to the end.

Repulsion

Repulsion is what happens when people are so dissimilar that there is no common ground of understanding, outlook, or experience, upon which to meet. They may feel some measure of repulsion or dislike towards each other.

This model isn't particularly profound. We can all relate to it. Its usefulness though comes with seeing it in black and white. Our subconscious minds often run agendas which are contrary to reality, and this causes stress and conflict for us. Remember that most of us seek to be accepted and/or esteemed by our community. This subconscious agenda creates feelings of "something is wrong" then when no esteem or acceptance is forthcoming. Often it can make us feel like there must be something wrong with **us**.

This model highlights that being liked/esteemed will only be possible with approximately two thirds of any community, those being the people we find ourselves attracted to, or in cohesion with. This is not a rigorous analysis. Variables will mean that the figure differs from situation to situation. If you're a pacifist at a weapons fair you're not likely to make friends, but even in everyday life, we can be sure that some percentage of those we come into contact with will be disharmonious with us in some way. In other words, you'll never please everyone, and not everyone will please you. This is as inevitable as the sunrise. Repulsion is unavoidable. It's going to happen sometimes.

In recognising this as **a fact of life**, we can move away from the perception that there might be something wrong with us personally if people don't warm to us. This is especially important to understand if you suffer with low self-worth generally because a meeting which results in some measure of repulsion may carry much more significance for you than it would for someone else. Some may hardly notice it. For you it might play on your mind persistently.

There are some personal subconscious agendas which can be corrected with good therapeutic adjustment but this is not really one of them. We are up against millennia of evolutionary programming here. This particular need to be accepted by all is not personal, it's collective. The correct position on this is to understand consciously that any feelings of "wrongness" from such an encounter are merely an echo from evolution. Experiencing repulsion with others doesn't really say anything about you or the other. I acknowledge that there are limits here. If you meet a violent psychopathic criminal and feel repelled, then maybe you have a case, but generally it's just that you're from different worlds. That **can** be viewed as value neutral. Easier said than done perhaps, but possible. This is the work of our lives.

Sometimes we can completely misread people too. This is a fact that some people may never be privy to. My experience as a therapist has helped me to understand a lot of things about the social dynamics in the world which are not common knowledge because many people don't reveal to others why they are the way they are. Some may not know themselves. One area where this is particularly relevant is in the field of social anxiety. You may yourself have personal experience of this?

Sometimes people come across as being unfriendly, aloof, or disinterested in us. In my personal life, I've experienced this, only to discover at a later date that the person in question actually has a rather anxious time being around other people. In the consulting room, I came to understand just how common this is. The thing is, people are often expert at hiding their discomfort, so someone who is socially anxious may not present as socially awkward, and that can be really confusing for the unsuspecting recipient as a vague sense that something isn't quite right is interpreted as a dislike or irritation. Some people feel strongly stigmatised about their anxiety and they may never discuss it with anyone.

The lesson to take away here, is that if somebody seems to be a bit aloof or distracted with you, do take a moment to ponder on whether they may actually be experiencing some social anxiety? Dealing with anxiety takes up a lot of space for the sufferer and they may be multi-tasking. Don't jump to conclusions that other-peoples' behaviour says anything about you. Sometimes it's not about you at all.

There are other ways that we can get people wrong too. My friend had a Swedish girlfriend. I really liked her and we got on well but I thought she could be rude sometimes, particularly when she asked for something. I noticed that she rarely (if ever) said "please", and it seemed conspicuously absent. I went on for quite a while thinking that she was abrupt at times before discovering that there is no exact match for the word please in the Swedish language. Instead, they offer gratitude in advance by ending their request with "Tack" which is "Thank you". Since English people don't generally say thank you during a request, when she translated to English, she left it off. Now, to an Englishman this sounds quite demanding. "Can I have one of your "X", thank you" appears to assume that the answer is already yes. My response is usually "of course you can" but I like to be asked rather than told. There was nothing at all wrong with her manners. They were simply lost in translation.

It is also my understanding that "losing face" is something to be avoided at all costs in many Eastern countries, and yet we Brits suck that stuff up as a form of entertainment. I'm not kidding. We call each other bad words as greetings and terms of endearment; friends only, of course! We also like to point out each other's faults. I know it's cheap but we like a bit of deprecation here and there. In Thailand, pointing your feet at people is an insult. Burping publicly after a meal is a sign of appreciation in some parts of the world. Even in our own culture, what some people take offence to, others don't. Intentions can be easily misread. Remember that we've all got different rulebooks, and what comes across as rude or hostile to you may just be the way that person rolls. Are you sometimes misunderstood? Is your heart in the right place? Maybe theirs is too?

Next up, we have the "Warriors, Settlers, Nomad" model. This is a wonderful psychological system developed by my friend, mentor, and teacher, Terence Watts. He proposes that Humanity can be roughly divided into three groups - Warriors, Settlers, and Nomads.

The Warrior is **resolute and organised**. The Settler is **intuitive and adaptable**. The Nomad is **charismatic and evidential**. In practice this means that Warrior types are go-getters with a no-messing approach. Settlers are soft, sharing, caring versatile problem-solvers, and Nomads love change, excitement, novelty, and fun.

This is a really useful model for understanding the people in the world. It once again highlights the inevitability of a certain degree of conflict. Nomads, for instance, are fun-loving and spontaneous by nature. How might this conflict with the resolute no-messing approach that a Warrior might have? Warriors don't suffer fools gladly, but Nomads are often the fulfilment of "the fool" archetype (freedom loving and playful). If a Warrior and a Nomad are on a work team together, there is the potential for them to complement each other. The Warrior will bring stability and focus, and the Nomad will bring the ideas. If it doesn't go so well, the Warrior might feel really irritated by the joviality of the Nomad and the Nomad will think that the Warrior needs to lighten up! Warrior types can sometimes be received as intimidating. Settlers can seem too weak and watery, and Nomads, fickle and shallow.

We can make the mistake of misjudging somebody's nature for their will.

Something well worth understanding, is that the body language of these different personality types can be confusing if you don't understand that they don't do things how you do things. If you think that your way is the "right" way, you're going to dislike two out of three people. There are no "right" ways. There are only different ways, and each is valid. All have their own talents. Warriors are likely to be stoic. Settlers will be agreeable. Nomads will be animated. Looking out into an audience when I've spoken publicly, I've seen nodding heads, smiling faces, and also stony expressions of what I took to be possibly contempt. "They hate me", I thought. Ever brave, I pressed on regardless. To my shock, the stony faces have often been the ones who have spoken to me later to say how much they enjoyed the talk! As they walked away, I had to pick my jaw up off the floor. That taught me something right there. People are hard to read sometimes.

Using this model, we can see that we are not merely carriers of different belief systems and values. We are actually fundamentally different in terms of our genetics and ancestry. A person doesn't choose their personality type. It's in their genes. All they can do is work to affect small changes in the experience and expression of their inherited personality.

A person isn't **wilfully** fun-loving and gregarious, or quiet and reserved because they choose to be. It's in their nature. No matter how much we might **want** to be naturally hilarious or Einstein genius, it's just not going to happen unless we were born to be that way. Gay people can't be straight. Straight people can't be gay. Introverts can't be naturally extrovert, black people can't be white, and white people can't be black. We are what we are. These are the facts, and yet some people still can't accept them.

With this in mind, we can begin to see how ridiculous judgement and prejudice is. How can we expect people to be something they are not? What is the point exactly of being upset by diversity? Diversity in the world is never going away. Either we adjust and get okay with this, or we get bitter and spread hatred. It seems like a no-brainer to me, but evidently there's still a lot of it about.

People still hate others for <u>what</u> they are rather than <u>who</u> they are!

I know that most of my readers won't have a problem of this nature, but I'm using this to illustrate the ridiculousness of a hateful position. Hate is drinking poison and then expecting the other person to drop dead. It's foolish. And the reason that I've framed this so strongly is because I'm about to present you with the finale...

If someone is hating on you for just being you, it's because there's something miseducated, wilfully ignorant, or wounded and bitter in them, not you!

I don't say this with any anger or malice towards the haters. I feel sad for them. They are missing out. Loving is nice. Behind most hatred is a terrible story somewhere down the line, an unacknowledged wounding, a betrayal, an environment of ignorance or malice, or a heart badly broken. Neither do I hold a position of moral superiority on this. I simply count myself lucky because I have lived in an environment which has supported the development of an inclusive worldview. I have also found the support necessary to examine my own personal rage, understand where it was coming from, and heal the wounding. As a result, I get to **enjoy** diversity instead of being freaked out by it. As one of the lucky ones who has tasted the transformative power of love and seen what it can do, I am compelled to fight for love in a world where hatred and division is often peddled as a solution to our troubles. While I don't see it as a morally superior position, I am willing to say that a loving world is a far superior **practical** vision for the world and our future. Hatred or division has never been a solution and it never will be. It can only ever bring pain. Unfortunately, those who have not tasted love will not understand this, and that's another good reason to continue standing up for it.

There are wards of tragedy inside prisons and hospitals filled with sadistic people who are beyond rehabilitation. There are people who really are bad to the bone and literally incapable of any mercy or compassion. Some are walking among us. Some might even hold positions of power.

Apparently, psychopathy has its roots in genetic traits, which when coupled with negative environmental influences (ie abuse), can lead to the development of behaviours that most of us would consider pure evil. I am not naïve to the realities of the world. Lasting world peace may well be unattainable. It almost certainly goes against the nature of reality since reality is dualistic. It contains opposites. There will always be good and evil, and even if peace were theoretically attained, there will always be some idiot born who decides to tear it down. History is a pendulum.

My point is, that those opposites don't have to be so extreme, and I believe that this is the real work that we are doing in the world collectively. We are becoming less extreme overall. Collectively we are moving closer to the centre. Historically, we've approached our disputes by blowing the planet, and each other, to smithereens; truly apes with weaponry. Most wars are eventually settled with discourse, compromise, and agreement, when we stop behaving like unevolved primates and step into our Humanity. Wouldn't it be better if we just skipped the war part and went straight to the negotiations? That is what I mean when I suggest that we avoid the extremities of polarity. Anything that can't be agreed upon after that should be settled with sports or karaoke!

I have no illusions of grandeur. I know I can't establish world peace, but my wish is simply to ease a little suffering wherever possible. My voice is no more than a whisper in a hurricane which some may hear, and others may reject. I know that. We will each do our little part in our own way, and this is one of the very best reasons to embrace the notion of loving yourself fully as a serious enterprise. If you want to do your bit in easing the suffering in the world, it starts with loving yourself. If we don't have love within us, it will be very hard to find it "out there", and even more difficult to have any to spare for anyone or anything else. There is Humanity beyond hate. Healing is possible, and love is the outcome.

If we owe it to the world, we owe it to ourselves just as much, and nobody has a right to deny that to us. If the haters are going to hate, let them hate. It says a lot more about them than it will ever say about you.

If beauty is in the eye of the beholder...then so is ugliness.

They're going to carry that heavy weight around with them until they let it go. It's their loss and it's their personal work to learn the hard way that their hatred will eat them up. Some will change, some won't. It's just a shame that the rest of us have to deal with the catastrophic consequences of their often wilfully slow education. I hope this information helps you to know right down to the core of your being why hateful opinions are not worth the air it takes to speak them. The haters may always be there. It's our job to get on with improving things anyway, and that includes learning to love yourself deeply.

Then, maybe, we can build it...and they will come.

This concludes our exploration of the conscious mind approach to self-love, and I hope it's helped. As a hypnotherapist however, the real substance of what I offer is in understanding the transformative power of the unconscious mind, and you're now primed to move on. You'll see the value of our previous discussions here once we reveal the tools and approaches which will, I hope, help you to experience a deep transformation in the way that you relate to yourself.

Chapter Sixteen – Acceptance

I asked some of my friends this question: -

What is loving yourself? And, what do you find the most difficult obstacle when it comes to loving yourself?

These are literally the first five responses, exactly as I received them: -

"Pushing beyond my failings in character after accepting them as part of me. For example, avarice and laziness, loss of motivation and action are a constant battle. How I find a way through is tricky, and I'm still looking!"

"For me, loving myself is about accepting myself exactly as I am, and knowing that I am worthy of my own love (and others' love) without having to change how I look. My difficulties have always been about learning to love my body. Learning that my weight or my size makes no difference to the beautiful soul inside! And, that's hard when we are constantly bombarded with messages that tell us that slim is beautiful and being overweight is definitely not!"

"For me, it's accepting the things I can't change and working on what I can change. I'm my own biggest critic when it comes to my artwork, often not starting a project because I lack self-confidence. Whenever I have a word with myself, I focus on the "journey" and what I've learnt, rather than the outcome. It's the same with relationships – I thought I needed someone else to feel good about myself but now realise that it's up to me to make myself the best I can be."

"For me, it's trying to accept that I do fail, and finding constructive ways to acknowledge and correct/move on from those failures."

"Loving myself is accepting who I am, warts and all. It is also allowing myself to prioritise my own needs because I am worth it...working on areas I want to improve, and accepting myself each day as the person I am."

The first thing that jumps out when you read these in sequence is a single word: **accept.**

Buddha said "Your suffering is caused by your clinging and your aversion".

Understanding the wisdom in that single sentence is a life's work. The basic understanding behind this quote is that we suffer when we try to hold on to that which we fear losing, and we suffer when we resist what we don't like.

The Buddhist solution to this problem is to work on cultivating more **acceptance** in meeting the world the way it is, instead of how we wish it would be. Facts are facts. Everything is impermanent and in a constant state of change. If we cannot meet this uncomfortable truth gracefully, then we will do so kicking and screaming.

Pain is pain, but suffering is pain resisted.

Making peace with things the way they are is what acceptance is all about.

So why is acceptance such a problem for us? Well, for starters, we in the west don't generally devote much of our lives to **cultivating** acceptance. The head in the sand approach is widely favoured.

Under the circumstances, we can't be blamed. Who actually cherishes the idea of willingly devoting time and energy to contemplating death, ageing, illness, unpleasant feelings, and loss?

These matters seem like an insoluble problem. There are limits to how much acceptance the average person can cultivate. Should we simply "accept" it when a loved-one dies, or we lose our most beloved property, or are suddenly struck down by a life-changing illness? During the writing of this book, I had the misfortune of experiencing a "dry socket" following a difficult botched tooth extraction, resulting in two weeks of the worst relentless physical pain I've **ever** experienced. There was sobbing. I did **try** to mindfully meditate on accepting the situation. I lasted about two hours before reaching for more painkillers. Like I said, there are limits!

But, let's not throw the whole idea out. Acceptance may be way too much of an ask for these more extreme life experiences but we also know that sometimes we over-react to the lesser ups and downs of life, and we know that our failure to get to grips with these natural undulations leads us into prolonged suffering. Acceptance is evidently on the radar for many people but we don't always know **how** to engage in a meaningful way to work on cultivating more acceptance.

If I were to tell you that acceptance is a skill, would that make you think differently about it?

Skill is the closest word I can find. It could also be called a habit. Let me explain. The human brain consists of a vast network of cells which connect to each other, and these cells constantly exchange data.

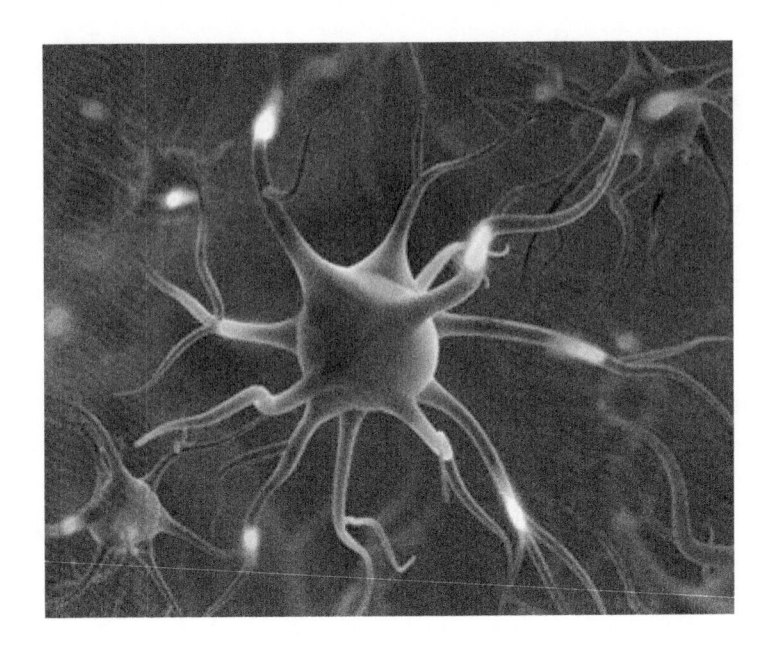

If the first thing you do in the morning is brush your teeth, then your brain cells already have an established pattern or pathway which allows that action to be undertaken pretty much without you having to think about it. You do it every day. Your brain therefore knows exactly how to make that happen. These are known as "neural pathways".

Neural pathways are like muscles. The more often they are used, the stronger they become. These are our habits. We can have good habits and bad habits, and the brain likes doing habits because they are easy. The brain doesn't particularly like having to form new patterns because doing so is difficult. That's called learning. Learning is difficult. It takes energy to learn, and most learning begins with confusion, which is stressful. Stress itself is unpleasant, and we naturally shy away from it. We mostly only bother to learn something new when there is something in it for us, even if that's only that we know we'll eventually enjoy it, or benefit from it, once we have mastered it. The act of learning itself isn't pleasant for most people. The reward of having learned it, is.

Acceptance itself is a quality which can be **cultivated**, that is, learned. In order to "learn" it, we must "practice" it. From a clinical perspective, a regular practice of acceptance will install new neural pathway circuits in your brain, so that when big changes or great discomforts do happen in your life, your brain actually has some way to process those events efficiently. There need be no great mystery as to why some people recover from emotional shock better than others. Preparedness counts. This is a case of prevention being better than cure.

Now, to put this idea of practice into some sort of perspective, Buddhists who are serious about this acceptance business, can and do devote much of their lives to the practice of cultivating (learning) acceptance. The goal of this learning is to be at peace with life's inevitable losses, and remain unimpressed by the acquisition of power, wealth, and accolades, thus sparing ourselves from a lifetime of servitude to ultimately empty pursuits. Money and status don't buy happiness or love, and neither do they insulate us from loss. Acceptance of life on its own terms is the only currency which will offer us shelter from the squally winds of change. By freeing oneself from the drama of desire and horror, we position ourselves to retain our emotional balance during times of turbulence, be they wonderful or awful. This is known as *equanimity*. Most therapy has similar aims.

We probably don't need to devote our entire lives to these matters to enjoy the benefits of cultivating acceptance. An illuminating study by the neuroscientist Richard Davidson, demonstrates that there are scientifically measurable results associated with the practice of meditation, and compassionate-attention exercises.

Interestingly, the research matter was suggested to Davidson by the Dalai Lama himself, who noted that we're very good at scientifically researching what's wrong with us, but rarely do we focus on what might be right. Seeing the potential in the idea, Davidson took a test group of experienced Buddhist monks into the laboratory, and hooked them up to MRI (brain) scanners. One of the participants described his meditation as "a state in which love and compassion permeate the whole mind, with no other consideration, reasoning, or discursive thoughts." He then asked the monks to switch from natural to meditative states, and recorded the results from the brain scans. He said, "When we did this, we noticed something remarkable. What we see are these high-amplitude gamma-oscillations in the brain, which are indicative of plasticity". Neural plasticity is the phrase used to describe the brain's ability to be flexible;

in other words, to be adaptable to changing conditions. In addition to this, findings also showed that the Insular Cortex within the brain was highly active in the monks. This part of the brain is hugely relevant in terms of cognitive-emotional processing, and has strong links to the body, orgasm, and the immune system. The left pre-frontal cortex, known to be active in problem solving mode, is also implicated. Theoretically then, meditators have less illness, more emotional balance, better problem-solving awareness, greater resilience to challenging conditions, and just for good measure, they apparently also have great sex!

In 2013, Davidson went on to test a group of everyday folks who had undertaken nothing more than a short "compassion training" meditation course. He found that this group were more likely to exhibit altruism (selflessness) than the non-meditative test group, so you can add kindness to that list of benefits too.

It is a mistake to believe that acceptance is something you either have or don't have. I am highlighting that it is a "skill", and skills must be learned (uurggh!) and practiced (double uurghh!) to be mastered. Yes, it's a drag. But here's the thing. How much pain do you experience in your life as a result of lacking acceptance? What do you rage against daily because you don't like how it is? What makes you feel like a failure because you haven't attained it? Are any of these things really that important when you analyse them? Or, are you being driven merely by emotion? Is it simply that you hope that the acquisition of that desired thing, or the destruction of something else you don't like will bring you peace? Will it? Really? In our heart of hearts, we know we're playing a losing game here. There's a reason that the grass is always greener on the other side. Neither acquisition, nor riddance, will bring us the peace we hope for because it's not out there…it's inside. Maybe, a short practice in the skill of acceptance here and there could save you a lot of pain in the long run?

That's all very nice you say, but how? Well, I'm always keen to provide the explanation, and some solutions, so let's move on to some practical understanding on how to cultivate acceptance. The first of these is easier than easy. In fact, it's not even going to be a task, only a pleasure!

As you may have gathered, I've been inviting people onto my hypnotherapist's couch since 2003. Typically, a session begins with a comfy couch, a nice supportive pillow, and a soft blanket for warmth, privacy, and comfort. We play some soft, soothing music in the background, I ask my client to close their eyes, and then I speak to them softly, using carefully constructed language patterns designed to soothe and guide them into a state of deep relaxation. Mostly, this would be used as a precursor to beginning some psychotherapeutic work such as investigating root-causes of wounding etc, but it can also be used purely for relaxation, and this can have great therapeutic benefits alone. In hypnotherapy, you are provided with positive suggestions which focus your mind on solutions and positive perspectives. Buddhists will undertake exercises such as (imagining) sending love and kindness to all beings. Hypnotherapy does roughly the same thing, though therapeutically it's usually focussed towards oneself. Some people get the horrors when they hear the word *hypnosis* but it's terribly misunderstood, and needlessly feared. Don't tell anyone I said this, but when used in this format for relaxation purposes, it's basically a lazy-person's meditation. It is to meditation what Thai massage is to Yoga. In Thai massage, someone else stretches and pummels your body. In Yoga, you do it for yourself.

As is customary with my books then, I am providing you with the easy-to-do method - another beautiful recording designed to assist you in absorbing the messages within this book. Go to the link provided below and either stream or download (recommended) the recording I have lovingly crafted for you. Put forty minutes aside, when and where you won't be disturbed, sit or lie comfortably in loose clothing, and play the recording with your eyes closed. You will enjoy a soothing relaxation recording, packed full of positive perspectives and suggestions for relaxing into acceptance and valuing yourself more deeply. You may be pleasantly surprised by the level of relaxation you are able to experience. I have had countless people tell me that they have never been so relaxed in their lives. I'm not promising that, but give it a go, and remember that your experience of relaxation is likely to deepen with practice. Do be aware that if you have any kind of negative reaction to using this recording, then you should discontinue use. It's there to help, not hinder. There's a disclaimer on the page which will explain. Most people will find it soothing and helpful though. Enjoy! And re-use as often as you wish.

Get your free recording at this link: -

https://www.youcanfixyouranxiety.com/inner-human-relaxation

The next item I'm going to share with you is a tool which is extremely powerful when used correctly. For readers familiar with my favourite methods, please forgive some of the overlap which you may recognise from other books here. It's unavoidable and necessary. Hopefully you'll also recognise the extraordinary flexibility of the approach though, as there are a few tweaks this time to bring us into line with the subject matter.

Acceptance is the absence of resistance. The practice of acceptance then, is the practice of learning to be in the presence of that which (usually) disturbs us. Without resistance.

Acceptance is essentially a conditioning process. You see, when we fear something, we keep it mentally at arm's length – out of our space, or at least, we try to do so. It doesn't work though because **what we resist persists**, and that material returns again and again because it seeks to be attended to. Our fears are asking for healing. If we ignore their calls, they'll continue to trouble us.

Suppose that I fear spiders. I'm always edgy because I might encounter one in the house. I can avoid spiders most of the time but the fear never goes away. The only way I can overcome that fear is to ultimately become comfortable in the presence of spiders. Spiders are not going anywhere. They are a part of the world. If I want peace, then I will need to change my response to them. In order to learn how to do this in the real world, I will need to allow myself the experience of having them close to me. One way to approach this therapeutically is to expose myself gradually, in manageable bite-size chunks. We recognise that this must be done gradually. If you throw yourself in the deep end, you may be likely to sink rather than swim. If we overwhelm ourselves by biting off too much all at once we run the risk of deepening our fear. If we approach such projects slowly however, there is every chance that we will succeed.

So, I might first spend twenty minutes just looking at a photograph of a spider. If I stick with this for long enough, my brain will begin to adjust. I might feel terrified initially, but over the twenty minutes which unfolds, my brain will begin to make an adjustment. By staying focussed on the image for a period of time courageously, and noting that no harm follows, my brain's alarm level will reduce.

In order to make a success of this, I am going to need to tolerate the initial feelings of discomfort. This is challenging, but not impossible. It may take a while, but eventually I will notice that my responses to the image of the spider have become considerably calmer. I may still not like the image but it won't be creating the same powerful, negative, visceral response that it did prior to my **willing** exposure to it. Next, maybe the next day, I might hold a plastic spider in my hand. If I spend another twenty minutes getting used to holding a plastic spider, the same process will happen again, leaving me feeling just a bit more comfortable with the presence of a spider. Then I may move on to being in the presence of a real live spider, perhaps safely underneath a glass initially, and sit very close to the spider, observing it, for another twenty minutes. Once I can do that without significant fear, I may be able to actually handle the spider physically without feeling any irrational sense of fear. Zoos often offer phobia courses which look very much like this, and by and large, they are successful treatments. This is known as "systematic desensitization", and it's a recognized form of therapy.

I'm not a great fan of reality TV shows but one I do have a fondness for is "I'm a celebrity, get me out of here!" This show invites a handful of celebrities to spend three weeks in the Australian jungle, sleeping outside on the ground, or in hammocks. They must earn their food supplies by successfully completing challenges which typically involve being locked in small spaces with bugs, snakes, rats, water, or even crocodiles. If they don't complete the task, they live only on meagre rations of unseasoned beans and rice for that day. Over a three-week period, we watch these polished celebrities face their worst fears, fall in and out of favour with each other, and re-discover their natural muddy wildness. They usually lose some weight too.

As a general rule, the participants leave the experience stating that it's been one of the greatest times in their lives, despite the severe hardship. They begin their three-week sojourn shrieking hysterically at anything which moves and end it as stoic fearless warriors of the wilds, capable of enduring all manner of bug-filled environments, and hunger, with little complaint. This show fascinates me, not for its sadistic value, but rather its transformative value. It has always struck me that this process is much like a group shamanic initiation. The participants are without significant distraction for many hours each day which leads to intense self-reflection and a clearer understanding of what is truly important to them. They experience hunger. They must unite and support each other to survive. They must become comfortable in nature. They find strengths they didn't know they had, and realise how irrelevant much of what they hold dear actually is. The letters from loved ones in week two is always a tear-jerker. If you doubt that systematic desensitization is really a thing, there is no greater proof than this particular show.

If you understand clearly how this process operates now, you will recognise that we can employ the same processes to become more acceptant of other factors within our lives. So, let's suppose that I have terrible feelings every time I make a mistake. My initial response to this, is to attempt to do everything perfectly from this point forwards thus avoiding the terrible feelings which are supplied every time I make a mistake. Clearly this is a situation which is going to continue to cause me pain though because making mistakes is human. They cannot be avoided. Remember, aversion is a cause of suffering. If I am going to cultivate peace in myself, I will need to train my body and mind to be comfortable in the presence of mistakes.

Here's what I am going to do. I'm going to put some time aside. This time is exclusively allotted to this exercise. I want to be fully present. I will now close my eyes and take a few nice deep breaths. Then I'll just allow myself to move into a quiet space by following the sensation of breathing in and out. I will expect that there will be some distractions. I may find that my mind wanders off to thinking about the shopping which I need to do later on, or I may find that there are other thoughts which arise. This is fine. I simply allow these thoughts to come and go without attaching to them, and return to noticing my breath every time I realise that I have drifted away from my breath-focus. I will do this patiently, and taking great care not to berate myself if I lose focus. Distraction is to be expected. If I remain gentle with myself, I will find that over a period of minutes, eventually, a clearer focus will emerge naturally and automatically, and on a good day I will find myself relaxing too. This simple barrier of distraction is the main hurdle to success with meditation. Westerners are typically impatient here and give up, saying they can't do it. Don't! This process may be unfamiliar, and you will experience strong urges to quit sitting around like a dumb hippy and get back to your busy-ness. That's your ego talking. It wants you to fail at this. The ego likes you to remain distracted and busy. It doesn't want you to realise there is a peace available beyond the discomfort because then it will be out of a job.

There was a cartoon floating around on social media recently which summed it up nicely. It said…

"You should meditate for ten minutes a day…unless you think you're too busy. Then you should make it an hour!"

This is the format used for the most basic form of meditation. Stay with it for as long as you need to. Be willing to be bored and frustrated for a bit. There is something beyond this immediate state of distraction. These feelings of discomfort and impatience are the actual default state for most human minds, and that's not a good thing. The reason we feel them when we sit down and do nothing is that when we are paying attention in this way, ignoring our usual stream of useless mind chatter, then these things come into focus. See these feelings of irritation as a good reason to be patient and make the effort. Remember, sometimes, nothing is something worth doing. If you simply stay with the process patiently, they'll begin to dissipate. You will only learn this by doing it. You're not looking for transcendental bliss. The outcome we're after is a little bit of settled time. That's all. Keep it simple.

Like the old Zen master said, "It is simple. The problem is, you are complicated."

Now, with my mind in a quieter place, I have the benefits of clarity. This makes it easier for me to tune in to what's going on for me at a deeper emotional level. For clarity, that means "what is going on inside my body at the **feeling** level".

Now I'm going to say the words, out loud, "I am okay with making mistakes". In this example, I know that this statement happens to be untrue for me (hypothetically, as this an example) and because it is untrue, I expect that my body will respond with a sense of anxiety or awkwardness. I will feel this somewhere within my body as I say those words. My body will register it as an untruth. This is a reverse-psychology method for bringing the fear or discomfort forward so that I can work with it consciously. I don't need to *make* this happen. It is automatic. My feeling body will counter this untrue statement with the truth. It will respond with what I **actually** feel. We already know what this is. This exercise simply allows us to create a meaningful connection with that feeling in the moment.

Now I will tune in on where that feeling of untruth is strongest, and I will take my undivided attention to that place within my body. Mentally, I will begin to focus wholly and completely on that feeling alone. If that feeling could speak for itself, it would be saying something like "I am **not** okay with making mistakes", or "I feel anxious about making mistakes." My job, here then, is to spend some time **being** in the presence of that discomfort without making a drama out of it, that is, without resistance. So, all I am doing here is being willing to sit and **witness** that feeling of anxiety or awkwardness without responding negatively to it. I'm just present with it, and remaining calm. Remember these two words - **being** and **witnessing**.

Pause for a moment. Think about this. What's happening here? Maybe for the first time in my life, I am not trying to keep those anxious feelings at arm's length. What message does this send back to my anxious self? Do you see the parallel with the spider example? I'm giving my brain time to calm down around this material, and adjust the response. Up until now, we've always made the adjustment by avoiding or escaping the feelings. Now we're doing the polar opposite.

If the usual message I send by trying to keep it at arm's length is that this material is so disturbing that it must be kept at bay, then my brain has no choice but to conclude that this theme of mistakes must be dangerous. If it is dangerous, then it must continue to be feared, right? That's the bind. Only by doing something differently can we initiate healing.

When you **willingly** sit with these uncomfortable feelings, you are changing your relationship to them. The act of sitting with them, basically says, "I am not alarmed". It is the act of sitting calmly in the presence of these disturbing thoughts and feelings, which tells the brain that they can't actually be that much of a threat, can they? This is the first step in minimising resistance and creating acceptance. This alone can be enlightening. We should experience a significant decrease in both the intensity and the urgency of the feelings.

We can go further though. With this simple practice, we have opened a dialogue. The feelings are now aware that we have noticed them, and that we are paying attention. This will usually deepen the experience. Now we can reach out with our heart.

The next step is to actually speak the truth, as it is. I am going to say, **out loud,** "I see/hear and accept that you feel afraid of making mistakes." And no, talking to yourself is not the first sign of madness. Speaking these words amplifies the message. Speaking resonates. I don't mean this figuratively. I mean it literally. Words have energy, particularly when they are spoken out loud. I'm suggesting that the speaking of those words, out loud, literally causes a physiological response. Sound is energy, and we are configured to understand resonant frequencies at a visceral level. We can be delighted or terrified by tone and intention, even if we do not actually hear the words themselves. You might feel alarm when you hear someone shouting in the distance. Sound carries information. Saying these words in a tone of sincerity and support is therefore crucial. This is a deep acknowledgment of what is, and your deeper self will "get it". To re-cap then, you speak the following words out loud with all the sincerity you can muster: -

"I see/hear and accept that you feel afraid of making mistakes."

Then just sit quietly and allow the words to resonate in the silence of the moment. They will echo mentally and emotionally in the silence. Pay attention to how your feelings respond. You should notice some sense of relief. The feeling that making mistakes is unbearably awful should begin to soften and dissipate. It doesn't need to be 100% relief. Just a small shift is great. Say it again. Remain sincere in your delivery. "I hear and accept that you feel anxious and afraid of making mistakes." Say it with heart. Project the feeling "I get it! I am fully witnessing your distress." Does it soften more? If it does, keep repeating with twenty to thirty seconds between each statement until there's no further shift in emotional response. Then you'll know you have done what you can for today. Come back at another time and run the process again. That's the definition of practice.

There is one further step which you may wish to use. Having now deeply witnessed and accepted the presence of your true feelings without judgement or avoidance, we can come forward with genuine empathy. Do you remember we discussed much earlier the notion of "original innocence"? If you can find it in yourself to connect with this understanding in this moment, you'll have a powerful ally. You never asked to be terrified of making mistakes, did you? Where did that come from? School? Parents? Employers? Peers? The inner critic? Somebody "dumped" that idea on you somehow. Somebody told you that you're not good enough if you make mistakes. Now you have an opportunity to truly connect with your recognition of your original innocence. See yourself as the loving, innocent person, that you really are, and set that broken record straight at the very deepest level of your being. Everything is in place. The communication channel is open. You are connected. Use this opportunity to speak the truth. What is that?

*"I'm really sorry that you've been made to feel that making mistakes is a terrible thing". Or, "I'm so sorry they made you feel bad about yourself when you made mistakes." Or "I promise you that you are **so** allowed to make mistakes, and I will not judge you for it!" Or, "I see your beauty whether you make mistakes or not. It's totally okay with me if you don't get everything right all the time."*

I could go on. The wording is less important than the intention. What message does your fearful/wounded-self need to hear? What do you want your truth to be? Let your heart speak with conviction and power, and your deepest self will hear it. If it is your truth, then it will be absorbed, and when it is absorbed it will change the way that you **feel**.

When you've done all that you can for today's session, just allow yourself to gently surface back to your normal waking awareness and close the exercise.

If you attempt these exercises and find that you experience no shift at all, that's okay too. I promise you that you have still done some good. Just because a part of you wasn't ready to be responsive yet, you have still demonstrated positive intention towards yourself. Come back and try again another time. There are many possible reasons why you may not be receiving any response from your feeling body. We're getting to those shortly, and when we've tackled those deeper resistances you'll find this process will play out very differently. As always, stay with me please.

As a final note on this chapter, here, I've used the theme of "making mistakes" in order to demonstrate the process. You will of course have your own particular areas of resistance to work through which are about something else entirely. The process will remain the same, but the wording will change. Simply replace the felt experience with the one which relates to your resistance. Instead of "I hear and accept that you feel...*afraid of making mistakes*", it may become "I hear and accept that you feel...*like you have an ugly body*" or "I hear and accept that you feel...*like a failure in life*".

If you don't already know specifically why you feel bad about yourself - worry not. In the next chapter, I'm going to explain how to go a little deeper into exploring the roots of your self-estrangement. You can come back to this exercise later with your new deepened understanding if that's the case. Just bookmark this section now.

These exercises, regularly practiced, can have a powerful transformative effect on your level of self-acceptance. Remember that apart from the obvious benefits of becoming a truly unconditional friend to yourself, you are also creating and strengthening neural pathways in the brain which will be set up and ready to go when unexpected hard times befall you.

There...now you know how to do "acceptance". You'll get back what you put in, so don't delay. Start today!

Chapter Seventeen - Getting To The Roots Of Your Feelings

Sometimes, we don't know why we feel bad about ourselves. I hope that the groundwork in the first half of this book has shone a spotlight into some previously unconsidered areas, but you may still be missing some vital information which relates to your **personal** situation.

Before I explain the method for uncovering your personal sticking points, I'm going to spend a little time laying out some foundations of understanding. It's a rule of psychology that people will only engage with something if they know **why** it's worth doing. What follows may seem academic. I have been accused, probably fairly, of being a bit too thorough on occasion, but I've always aimed to teach, not preach. Give a person a fish and all that. I really want to make you the expert here, so that you can "own" the process. A little attention now will make the world of difference to your experience when you come to put the tools to use, and I know that when you make this knowledge your own, it has the potential to completely transform the way that you relate to yourself. I'll keep it in plain English and as short as possible!

We live consciously on the surface of our awareness. We feel feelings, but we don't regularly recognise their deeper source, and it seems natural then to take them at face value. The work I am about to introduce you to may best be described as learning to be emotionally **intimate** with yourself. If we live with ourselves only on the surface, we may never really understand the deeper motivations which drive our feelings. Socrates famously said "The unexamined life is not worth living." He was apparently choosing between death and exile at the time, so his passion was understandable. Putting it more softly perhaps, we can say that there is value in understanding how we're wired.

We may know our conscious selves well but still be strangers with our unconscious selves. If this sounds mysterious, then let me use a fictional example to illustrate how the unconscious mind can create confusing feelings which have little or nothing to do with the problem we **appear** to have.

Sally is thrifty. She spends hours scanning and cutting out coupons from local newspapers, and she shops exclusively where there are bargains to be found. She finds it incredibly difficult to walk into a shop and buy anything for full price. She goes thirsty on a long walk rather than pay the local shopkeeper's rate for a bottle of water. She's proud of her economic skills and she says it's because her Mum was poor when she was growing up, and she has a deep respect for the value of money. This is her **conscious** explanation for her anxiety around spending money and her subsequent behaviours. She never gets beyond this.

A respect for the value of money is all reasonable enough of course, but that's only what's on the surface. Is it reasonable to deny yourself water when you're thirsty to save a few pennies? Or, to have to chase around from store to store for hours on end? Sally tells herself that she's okay with the arrangement, even though it takes up significant time, and makes her anxious sometimes. How can thrift be a bad thing, after all? But, there's something more to this story. She is being driven by an **unconscious** agenda which she is not fully aware of, and it's not about growing up poor. Actually, Sally has a great job and she's far from poor these days.

So, what is it really about? Let's suppose that Sally walks into the consulting room and explains that she is anxious about spending money, and it's making her life difficult. My job is to uncover the root of this anxiety, help her to heal, and disable any limiting belief systems which are negatively affecting her life.

I ask her to lie on the couch. We spend ten minutes or so bringing her into a state of deep relaxation and I ask her to remember the feeling she gets when she pays full price for something, and then describe it to me.

"It's like fear", she says. "Go on…", I reply. "It feels like something terrible will happen as the money leaves my hands…like I don't want to actually hand it over." I now ask her to tune in on **that terrible feeling** and describe it. She is silent for a few moments and then she suddenly bursts into tears. "I can see my Dad walking out of the door. He's leaving…he's LEAVING!"

What on earth could money have to do with her Dad leaving? It may sound strange, but the symbolism of something "valuable" **leaving** her has been "associated" with money. What she is actually seeing is a devastating memory from her childhood when her Dad left the family home, never to return. The subconscious rule which was created as a result of the event is that things of "value" must be held onto tightly. The pain of her loss has not been fully faced and integrated. Money becomes an analogy, and somehow gives her another shot at **avoiding** the "loss". I know it's weird, but it's just how it works in practice.

This is pretty typical of a day in the life of a therapist. The financial thrift is just a cover - a smokescreen. As long as Sally keeps doing thrift, she doesn't have to identify or deal with the real pain. **Thrift represents control over the uncontrollable**. She doesn't do this **consciously**. It's not a choice. This is the way the subconscious mind operates. It wants to keep us safe from old pains, and symbolically, holding on to money represents having some **control** over something symbolically valuable to her. Her Dad walking out she couldn't control. Money she can. Hoarding will often have similar roots.

To cut a long story short, from this moment in Sally's therapy, we go on to bring about some deep healing in short order. We help her to release the pain of the trauma, as we "witness" it with her, and she finally allows herself to fully recognise her true feelings around the loss, from the safety of a different time. We encourage her to connect with, and comfort, her wounded inner-child. We open a dialogue with her younger self, and we explain to her that we understand her pain. We explain that things are different now, and ultimately, we re-frame her relationship with money.

We have literally disconnected those feelings of anxiety and loss from the symbolic stand-in, money. Never again can she be hoodwinked by the illusion that those terrible feelings are about spending money. That has been proven to be a fiction by the revelation of the true root of those terrible feelings, and it cannot therefore claim her again. She is now free to spend money as she wishes, without anxiety. She may still choose to be thrifty, and that's fine, but she'll be doing it because she wants to, and not because she has to.

The subconscious mind is a strange thing. It really does make these kinds of erroneous connections. Knowing this, will help you to push beyond what you **think** is the problem, and move into a deeper connection with what might really be holding you back from loving yourself.

I should point out that the example given above is deliberately abstract because I wanted to illustrate how resistance is not always rational. Many people, however, will have a reasonable idea of why they feel a lack of self-love. Neglectful parents, brutal schooling, an abusive partner, a traumatic event, a physical or mental impairment, bullying, or even just plain bad luck could be among the reasons that a person might have lost touch with their ability to like themselves. I can tell you from experience though, that just occasionally, the source of your distress is not what you think it is, and it pays therefore to resist the temptation to assume that your initial assessment of the source of your pain is correct. The intellectual mind can create a cover story, as we saw with Sally. Remember how she told herself her thrift was because she grew up in a poor household and it turned out to be about her dad abandoning her? Yes. That.

The answer to the question of why we might find it difficult to be loving towards ourselves may not be in the **thinking** mind. It is much more likely that we will find it in the **feeling** body, and the good news is, that it really isn't very difficult to do so at all...once you know how. And you actually do know how, because I've already shared the basis of the tool we're going to use, with you. We just need a little tweak here to re-purpose this technique.

In the last chapter I explained how the body will respond powerfully when you speak an untruth. In that chapter, we used the statement, "I am okay with making mistakes". The outcome was that my feeling body revealed that this statement was incongruent with my truth and supplied me with the opposite feeling. From there, I was able to work on creating acceptance around the true feeling, which was, "I feel anxious about making mistakes". If you practiced this successfully already, you'll have a feel for how the process works. If not, let me add a little further explanation.

The truth matters. If somebody tries to tell you that black is white, you will immediately feel a strong sense of resistance to their assertion. Your feeling body will supply you with powerful sensations which carry the denial of the obviously untrue assertion, and often, this will include a retort too – sarcasm is not uncommon here. Our feeling bodies may not register a strong feeling towards something which might be arguable, but if something is definitely not true (such as black is white) then it's usually a pretty clear-cut feeling which springs forward. This therapeutic tool capitalises on this simple reaction. In essence, we are going to deliberately speak untrue words (a suspected lie), and then pay attention to the denial and retort which our feeling body will automatically provide.

The truth about the source of our inability to love ourselves will be found within that response/retort.

To begin with then, as in the acceptance exercise, take a few minutes to settle yourself into a clear, quiet, calm, state of awareness with your eyes closed, and ensure that you have allocated some undisturbed time exclusively to this exercise. When you have a sense of stillness and/or focus, imagine yourself sitting in the most inviting safe space you could imagine. It could be somewhere you know from real life, or it could be somewhere you create in your own mind. This will now be your safe space. Yes, I know this is an old cliché, but it works, and it's there for a reason. If you become uncomfortable with any part of the exercise, for any reason, you will simply return to this place in your mind's eye, re-centre yourself, take a few minutes to disengage from the work, absorb some calm feelings, and close the exercise on a peaceful note. It's just our way of ensuring that your exercises are safe and comfortable.

Before you proceed from here please note the following important points.

This book is designed to help you, and I want you to use it safely. I do not want you to re-experience any past traumas or dredge up any difficult emotional material. This technique is carefully designed to avoid doing so. If you do have a history of trauma, abuse, or mental illness, or feel that you are of a particularly fragile mental/emotional disposition, then I would suggest that you sit this technique out, and consult a professional therapist to help you work through that material in a **supported** environment, if you wish to do so. Please ensure that you have read, and agree to, the disclaimer at the front of the book before using this technique: -

If you are in agreement with the terms of the disclaimer, and are confident that you are of suitable mind and health to proceed safely, then, we'll move on. If you don't want to do the exercise/s, just read on and take what you can from the understanding presented.

You may be familiar with the idea of positive affirmations? For anyone who isn't, this is the practice of speaking a positive suggestion, out loud, with the intention of making it one's truth. So, for instance, I might decide that I feel too tired to exercise today. A positive affirmation to counteract this feeling might be, "I am strong. I am willing. I am capable. I will feel energized once I have done it. I am choosing to exercise today!" When using a positive affirmation, the idea is to say it with determination. You are affirming something after all.

The exercise we're about to use has an **entirely different agenda**. The words you are about to speak are not intended as affirmations, and should be spoken in a **neutral tone**. They are akin to an indirect question. The agenda here is to ask your unconscious mind whether it believes you are loveable, but we don't ask that question directly because that sometimes introduces pressure or doubt as a result of "trying" to know something.

Instead, we allow the mind's natural inbuilt "lie-detector" to do all of the work for us. When you speak the words in a neutral tone, with the intention to merely say the words and then **notice** (not try!) whether they are **felt** to be true, you will, more often than not, receive a pretty clear signal, one way or the other.

So, when you are in your prepared quiet space, you simply speak out loud the following words once, (or a few times if necessary) in a neutral tone, to get the process rolling: -

"*I am loveable*".

Now just pay careful attention to what happens in your body. If the statement is believed to be true by your unconscious mind (and it may well be), then you will experience either neutral feelings or perhaps even some pleasure in remembering that you are loveable. You may notice that your head nods involuntarily. This is a sure sign that the words you just spoke are considered to be true by your unconscious mind. You can more or less trust that you now have an accurate assessment of whether you believe that you are loveable or not, at the core level. In this case, since you received a neutral/positive feeling, then yes, you do believe yourself to be loveable. Great work. This is a thumbs up from the unconscious mind. You should have no problems in accepting kindness and love when it's shown to you, and you have a solid foundation for acting lovingly towards yourself, and being able to absorb and accept the kindnesses you extend to yourself.

If this statement is believed to be very **untrue** by your unconscious mind however, you will be immediately aware of a feeling (usually anxiety, frustration, sarcasm, disbelief, pain, or anger) which springs forwards in some way to tell you that what you just said is **not** congruent with what is believed at your core level. This is your unconscious mind's/body's way of saying that you just told it that black is white. The inner lie-detector has been triggered. You'll know. It will be quite definite. If you generally have a hard time being kind to yourself, you can expect that this is the likely response you'll experience.

Now, locate where you experience that sensation/feeling of untruth (your chest, belly, throat, head etc?), and offer that feeling your undivided attention. Take every bit of your available awareness to that place in yourself where that feeling resides. Feel into that feeling (the untrue feeling), and imagine diving into it as if you were exploring it from the inside. Notice what feelings or qualities exist inside the feeling. Do you sense anger, sadness, fear, or rejection? Do you feel a sense of futility, or of being crushed in some way? It really could be any feeling. Just pay attention, and without any urgency whatsoever, just be **curious** about the feeling. If you are curious, you are non-threatening. You are not responding emotionally. You are just taking notes!

Permit your mind the freedom to **be present** with the feeling/s and continue to pay attention. A picture, or knowing, will soon begin to develop. You might find the feeling connecting with a person, or a time, or an event. Don't try to force it. Just sit willingly and calmly with the feeling, and let it tell you its story, if it wishes to.

As the story begins to emerge, you imagine the story playing out on a piece of paper on the floor in front of you, which is no larger than a postcard. Imagine rising above it until it is so small that it evokes no emotional response at all. **This step is very important.** This is how we ensure that you don't re-experience the person/time/event in any upsetting detail. We do not need to do so, and we do not wish to do so. You want to remain calm and centred throughout the exercise. This "rising above" technique is an NLP-style tool used to create plenty of distance from traumatic material. Please ensure that you remember this step. All we need is an understanding of where your lack of self-love/worth originates from. Once we have that, we can close the session. The details of the connected time, events, or people, you already know consciously, and we don't need to review them in any way here, so please do not go back into the memories in any detailed way. Remain in a "detached observer" position. Don't re-ignite it, re-experience it, or ruminate on it. We just need a quick overview from a distance to be able to say "Ah...that's where these feelings root back to."

So, what is the story? Were you bullied at school? Did your parents treat you poorly? Were you abandoned? Did somebody make an innocent comment which got to you somehow? Did you lose your self-esteem after a relationship ended? Did you have an abusive boss? Did a partner abuse you? Did a business fail? Did you lose a bet? Did you hurt someone? Did you hurt yourself? Did you make a terrible decision somewhere? Did you have an anxious parent who taught you to be a doormat in life?

As soon as you have located the source of your negative feelings, you return to the safe place in your mind, and spend a few moments absorbing the peace of that space before bringing the session to a close, opening your eyes, and feeling good.

If your exercise has been successful you will now know "why" you have feelings of low self-worth.

Next, sit down with a pen and paper and record what you remember about that time/event/relationship. Don't upset yourself by over-thinking it or going into emotional rumination. Just identify the facts with a journalistic detachment. Specifically, answer the following questions: -

1) **What actually happened?** Was something specific said? Did somebody behave in a way which made you feel de-valued? Were there circumstances in which you felt powerless? Did you make a mistake which you've found it hard to forgive yourself for?
2) **How did it make you feel?**
3) **What conclusions did you draw about yourself at that time?**
4) **Looking back with the wisdom of years and greater understanding, how might you now look at that situation if you could go back in time and explain it to your younger self?**
5) **If somebody you cared deeply for told you this story, what would you want to tell them?**

With these answers in hand, we are now going to take another journey inside.

Return to your "safe space" in your mind's eye and spend a few minutes absorbing the peace of that place until your body and mind feel reasonably settled. Then, imagine "calling" for that younger self to join you here. Imagine him or her (we'll stay with "her" for explanatory purposes) travelling through time to be with you in this safe space. When she arrives, invite her to sit close to you. Be super gentle. No forcing or coercing at any time. Kindness, sincerity, and patience are key here. We definitely don't want her to feel judged or pressured in any way. If she will sit right beside you, that's preferable, but if she needs space, that's fine too. Let her sit as close to you as she is comfortable with.

Now we want to open a dialogue. Begin by taking at look at her. How does she look to you? Does she look beaten down? Is she angry, resigned, hateful, sad, afraid, ashamed, or hurt? If you can't "see" her clearly, perhaps you can "sense" how she feels instead? Failing that, you can try simply asking her how she is doing, and then listen for the answer. Since she has joined you from "that time", she carries the feelings which correspond with the upset which was present in that time. Trust that one way or another you'll get the picture.

We can open our dialogue with her with a truly empathetic statement which deeply acknowledges her pain. I recommend that you speak it out loud.

"I get (understand) that you feel really (X – whatever she is feeling)." Here, we'll use "worthless" for illustration purposes. "I am sincerely sorry that you've been feeling that way for so long."

So, that's going to sound like this: -

"I understand that you feel worthless. I am sincerely sorry that you've been feeling that way for so long".

Then, just wait, and watch. Normally, she will begin to brighten up. The very act of being deeply witnessed is often enormously soothing. This is step one – a simple but sincere, compassionate acknowledgement. Remember, no coercion or force is required. Say it with love, and gently repeat the message a few times, as feels appropriate. The message will eventually get through. You'll know when it has because she'll start to look or feel differently (typically anywhere from 10 seconds to a couple of minutes).

Once you've connected with her in this way, you can deepen the dialogue. Thinking back to the questions you answered on paper a few minutes ago, what is the message you want her to hear? This is the same message you wrote down in response to "what would I tell a friend?" and "how would you explain this if you could go back in time?"

When you deliver this message, you do so with all the love and power you can muster. You are speaking from your deepest heart to your deepest heart. This is a moment for absolute sincerity. There has been a terrible misunderstanding along the way. This is your moment to set that straight, once and for all. The three essential components to your self-talk are as follows: -

* *Her feelings should be fully acknowledged and validated.*

* *Explain to her clearly, using language which a child can understand, how and why there has been a mistake or misunderstanding which has led to the formation of these erroneous feelings about herself. Offer another way to see the situation in which she can feel kindness towards herself.*

* *Offer your ongoing support to make sure that she knows that you are on her side from hereon in!*

This might sound something like this: -

"I'm really sorry that the other children at school called you horrible names, and that being on the receiving end of that made you feel **worthless** *sometimes. I know that it's been really hard to ignore what they said and did to you, but you know what? There could have been so many reasons that they were like that. Some of them probably had horrible parents who treated them badly and they were just being horrible to other people because they were hurting inside and didn't know how to be nice anymore. They were probably horrible to lots of people, not only you. Some of them were just trying to fit in and avoid getting bullied themselves, so they only pretended to be horrible because then the bullies left them alone. Some of them were jealous of you because you're clever and they didn't feel clever themselves, so they thought they might feel better if they made you feel bad. But, whatever their reasons for calling you those names, I promise you...**I promise you**, that it had absolutely nothing to do with who you are, and **everything** to do with who they were! It was never about you. It was always about them. You don't have to feel sorry for them. You don't have to forgive them if you don't want to, but it's really important that you know that it was **always** about them, not you.*

You are anything but worthless. You are more valuable than I can express to you. I see your beauty. I see your innocence. And, I see your bright shining heart. I see your kindness, your generosity, your playfulness. I see you, and I think you're amazing! I want you to know that from this moment forwards, *forever now…I am here for you…and I'll never let anyone make you feel that way about yourself ever again. I want you to know that **I've got your back!**"*

If you have delivered this message with great sincerity, she **will** receive it. You will see her transform before your eyes. Her body language will shift. Her smile and confidence will return. Her fear will diminish. If she's not quite there yet, you can ask her, "Do you believe me?" If she looks unsure, you can continue the dialogue explaining upon whatever she is unsure about or needs to know. She might say, "But, I DO have a big nose!" Respond intuitively with kindness. I might reply that noses come in all shapes and sizes, and one size or shape isn't any better or worse than another. I might tell her that beauty is in the eye of the beholder and if people think she's ugly, that's because they are sad in themselves. I might tell her that some of the most attractive, admired and respected people in the world have larger noses than most. I will definitely tell her that her face is absolutely perfect to me, that I love her nose just the way it is, and it's what makes her who she is. That approach may, or may not be a good fit for you. Use your own words. You know what she needs to hear.

When she's absorbed your message fully, and is looking happy (happier is good enough!), thank her for spending this time with you, and explain that she can go back to her own time now, taking her new-found confidence with her. Tell her you are here for her at any time. Say your goodbyes and imagine her skipping back through time to her own time and space, resting there with a completely new outlook.

Now, here's where (I hope) you'll have your mind slightly blown, in a nice way of course. In your own time and space, now say the words that we used when we opened this exercise up. Do you remember them?

"I am loveable". Say it out loud.

Now, pay attention. What happens inside your body?

Assuming that the exercise went to plan, you should be experiencing a minor miracle! You should find that when you speak the words "**I am loveable**", it now **feels** true! There will be less anxiety, less resistance, less doubt. Your head may nod in agreement. It may feel no less true than speaking your name and date of birth. It's just a simple fact. "I am loveable." Yes, of course you are. You always have been. It's just that now your unconscious mind knows it as a fact too. Congratulations. You have just liberated yourself from a lifetime of baggage. This will last. This is not merely a "fix me up for a day or two" solution. Successful completion of this process will shift how you feel about yourself at a fundamental level. Try saying "I am loveable" a week from now. You'll almost certainly still get the nod.

If the exercise has not yielded these results for you, worry not. You will certainly have done no harm by bringing compassion and kindness to yourself. There may well be reasons that your unconscious mind is not quite ready to fully relax just yet, and we're about to move on to explore these areas now. Again, move along with the book, and when you've completed these later exercises, you can come back to this, and I'm sure it will unfold much more smoothly and deliver the positive results detailed here. If you did get the positive results first time, equally, stay with what follows. There may still be more you can do.

Chapter Eighteen - Self Forgiveness

We are all trying to forgive ourselves. We've all done things we're not proud of. Many of us have one or two dark secrets we may never tell anyone.

A few years ago, a friend and I stumbled into a spontaneous "ultimate confession" conversation. I don't remember exactly how it happened, but we told each other everything. We spilled the stuff we feared anyone ever knowing about us. I don't particularly recommend this, by the way, it just happened. It was fine with us. We've been friends since we were babies, and through so much together that these revelations were small potatoes in the scheme of things.

I relate this because there are two interesting insights which remain with me from that event. The first, is that when I actually told my secrets out loud (now you're wondering eh?), they didn't sound as bad as I felt they were, and he was far from shocked. The second, is that I genuinely have absolutely no memory of what my friend told me about himself. I remember thinking at the time "Wow, that's heavy. I can understand why you wouldn't want anyone to know that", but as for what he actually told me, I genuinely don't remember. It obviously wasn't so terrible that it stayed with me, and it has not made an ounce of difference to how I feel about him. That says a lot about us as people and as friends. In a different context, with the wrong person, I'm sure the outcome would be far less peaceful, but here's my point - my friend and I were far more forgiving of each other's pasts than we were of our own. As I hope we've established by now, we humans are our own worst critics.

Let's begin this chapter then, with some recognition that we all have regrets. What matters is where we are now, and perhaps most importantly, what we intend to do from this point forwards. If you have no intention of learning from your mistakes, then seeking self-forgiveness will be most likely be fruitless I'm afraid, for reasons I am about to explain. If you're reading this book, then I suspect your heart is in the right place, so rest assured there is hope yet.

You live with yourself every day, and all the secrets you carry, are known to yourself. There's nowhere to hide from that. We can come to a sense of relative peace with our past by recognising that what's done is done and that the past cannot be changed, but we often live in a state of resignation about this. It may be buried, but it's still present. Resolution is better.

However brilliant we are at consciously forgetting our past, if we carry a belief that we deserve to pay for our crimes at an **unconscious** level, then our well-being can become seriously undermined. We may believe that what we've said, done, thought, or been, is somehow unforgivable. When this happens, our toxic shame can remain ever-present at an unconscious level, affecting how we think and feel in every moment.

Whether you are aware of this fact or not, toxic shame limits the degree of happiness you permit yourself to experience. The level of shame you carry in your being relates directly to how "deserving" you believe yourself to be. If you feel like you are a bad person, then your unconscious mind is going to shut you down as soon as you start to get happy because as far as it's concerned, you don't deserve to be happy. If you've got an "unforgivable" agenda playing out at the unconscious level, then the never-ending verdict will be that you still haven't paid enough for your crimes. If it's a strong agenda, I cannot begin to express just how powerful this mechanism can be in making you miserable in life.

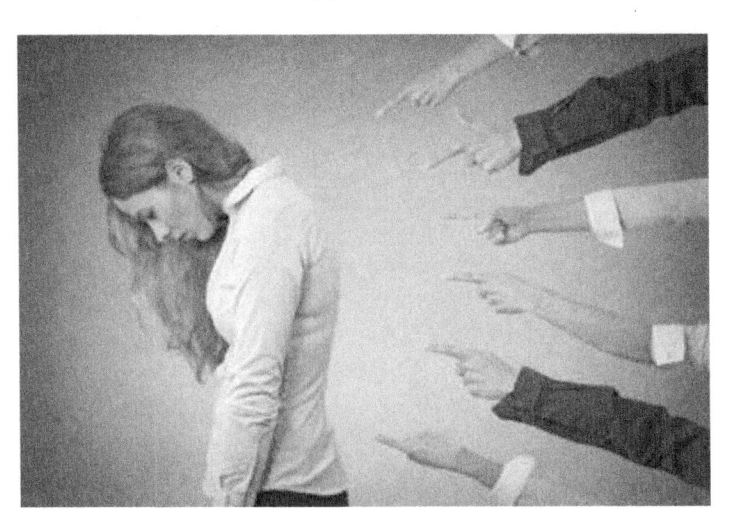

If you're familiar with my other books, you will know that I went through a severe and protracted period of anxiety and depression in my twenties which proved to be highly resistant to treatment.

The resolution and healing began when I worked with a particularly enlightened therapist, and the work we did together covered a great deal of ground which specifically tackled these "undeserving of happiness" blocks. Without doubt, one of the most important pieces of the recovery process, for me, related to self-forgiveness. I don't suggest that everyone has major blocks in this area, but I think many of us have something going on around these matters, so this is information worth knowing.

There were two outstanding therapeutic events which led to healing for me, one of which I shared in my book "Dear Anxiety – This Is My Life", and another which has remained private until now. A quick outline from Dear Anxiety is that during a therapeutic session, I experienced a spontaneous "past life regression" where I remembered having committed a crime of passion murder within a love triangle in ancient Egypt. I fell to my knees and begged forgiveness of the murdered man. A profound conversation ensued, and I was able to finally begin the process of challenging my unconscious assumptions that I was "unforgivable". I stated in the book that this may well have been a metaphorical experience relating to the fact that I had caused myself great suffering (in this life), rather than an actual past life experience. Nonetheless, it was a powerful event, and it certainly had great relevance to me as an individual. The therapist I was working with handled the situation with real expertise.

The second event unfolded with my next, and final, therapist. It was some months later. At this stage, my therapist and I had already succeeded in largely piecing me back together into some semblance of a functioning human being, and a detailed story of cause and effect had emerged. I was still struggling with intense feelings though and during this particular session, I was confronted by a powerful image. In my mind's eye, I saw my young self from some years earlier, laid out on a mortuary slab. It was quite a shocking image. I continued to look squarely at it and experienced the poignancy of the loss from many angles. I felt the sadness of the waste of precious life. I felt the anguish of my loved ones, and rather than it being anxiety provoking, it was actually just incredibly sad.

I felt sorry for their loss, and I felt sorry for my own. The image was at once a rendering of what could have been, and a metaphor for what I had been through. Where I had been experiencing deep depression and paralysing fear over the preceding years, I now became aware of a pervasive sorrow which was neither anxiety nor depression. The word which describes the feeling perfectly is that it was **sobering**. I somehow understood that my psyche was not showing me this image to shock me, or for dramatic value. It was much more matter of fact than that. This was a fate I had narrowly escaped, and I understood this more clearly in that moment than ever before. This could never happen again.

The feeling which sprung forth from me automatically then, was simply, "I'm sorry. I'm sorry for my decisions. I'm sorry for my mistakes. I'm sorry I didn't know how to take care of myself. I'm sorry I didn't listen to the parts of myself who were frightened by my life path. I'm sorry I took myself unknowingly to the brink of death."

There is much more I could tell you, but here's the essence of the message.

I needed to apologise to myself.

In the moments which followed, I offered myself the most heartfelt apology I knew how to express. I wasn't grovelling or begging forgiveness anymore. The drama was almost over. I'd come a long way in my therapy and this apology wasn't a desperate "Pleeeease release me. I'm sorry I screwed up!", to get me off the hook. It had an altogether different quality. It didn't even matter if I got anything out of it. It was just the right thing to do in the moment. It was a deep and reverent apology. I got it. I mean I really saw what had happened, and I just said it. "I am so, so sorry." I was. And, I knew then, that my apology had been deeply received, and the intention to make me pay endlessly for my perceived crimes finally softened.

I also made a promise then. I promised that I would never knowingly place myself in such a position again. This is a promise I have considered sacred, and have kept to this day. I consider it a condition of continued wellness.

That's my story, and I've shared it here to illustrate what a deep and meaningful conversation with your unconscious mind, your deepest self, your woundedness, your inner human, call it what you will, can actually look like.

If you've struggled with any of the exercises presented so far, there's a strong possibility that you may be suffering from a lack of self-forgiveness, and this may be why you've been unable to accept kindness from yourself. You may feel that you simply don't deserve it?

Contemplate this for a moment. If you have estrangement in any of your relationships, what is it that you want most from the other person? Isn't that some recognition of the way you've been hurt, and an apology? What would it feel like if that person were to soften and acknowledge your pain with a heartfelt apology? Would you stay angry at them? I know it depends on the scale of the betrayal. An apology doesn't right all wrongs, and there are people who you may wish to remain apart from even if they did supply a sincere apology. That's fine. In many instances though, you'd probably find your anger melting away.

When it comes to the relationship you have with yourself, there's nothing better than being your own best friend, and there are plenty of reasons to find the best in yourself and start liking what you see. You'll be spending the rest of your days with yourself, so if there was ever a relationship worth working on, it has to be this one. The price of reconciliation might be as little as an apology, and a promise. Nobody goes through life without making mistakes, and forgiveness often involves compromise, even if that means agreeing to disagree, and shaking hands anyway. A new conversation can be had another day if necessary.

If you wish to work on forgiving yourself, the format is quite similar to the previous two exercises. The usual disclaimer applies, and you can begin by getting yourself settled with eyes closed as before. In the first example, we're looking at self-forgiveness which relates to having done something we regret to someone, or something, else.

If you know specifically what you wish to work on in terms of self-forgiveness, then you can be specific in your statement. If not, just use a full spectrum statement such as "I have forgiven myself in life".

For illustration. let's say that I feel like I'm a bad person because I bullied a kid at school. To get to the "resistance" or "untrue" response I want to work with in my body, I'm going to say the opposite of what I know is true, as explained earlier. I speak the following words out loud.

"I have forgiven myself for bullying Mark X at school".

I just wait, and watch. I notice what happens in my body. Do I get a nod which tells me I have forgiven myself, or do I feel some tension arising? Has my chest or throat suddenly tightened? Do I hear a loud "No", or a sarcastic "Yeah...right!"? What signals come back to me when I speak those words? If I receive a nod, and a neutral or affirmative response in my body, there's a strong likelihood that this issue is already settled. If there's tension or resistance, then there is work to do.

I now tune in to that resistance or tension. How does it feel? I feel into in with curiosity. What feelings are inside of it? In this instance, I'm likely to feel disgust or shame, but it could be any feeling. Whatever I encounter, my first job is to sit with that feeling and witness it deeply. I will now say:

"I hear and accept that you feel really ashamed that you caused that boy pain. I know that you feel like you are a bad person".

The key at this point is now to **feel into your sense of regret.** Is your regret sincere? Regret is a difficult emotion to be present with, but be brave here because that feeling of regret carries within it the seeds of forgiveness. The fact that you have regret is your key to forgiveness. This is a moment of real honesty. I let myself feel the emotion of "Yes...that was bad. I deserve to feel ashamed...and I **do**!" Then, it is **deeply** acknowledged. This is simply the truth. I'd prefer it if it wasn't but that's what happened, so I must be willing to fully acknowledge how bad I feel about it.

Would I bully someone again today, knowing what I know? Hell, no! I've suffered in life. I've been on the receiving end of bullying. I know what it's like. Have I changed? Yes! Absolutely! I know this consciously, but remember that this aspect of myself, who is feeling that he is unforgivable, is still just twelve years old. I need to open a dialogue with him. I say,

"I know that you feel that what you have done is unforgivable. I get that you don't feel like you deserve forgiveness, and yes, what happened there was horrible, but there's something I need you to know. The past cannot be changed. What is done is done. I also know how sorry you are. I know that you would not do it again, and you know that too. There is absolutely nothing to be gained now by continuing to punish yourself because that will only make you feel bad, and that will make you more stressed, and therefore more likely to be mean to someone else, which is exactly what you don't want to happen, right? You don't get to be a better person by punishing yourself indefinitely. You get to be a better person by learning from your mistakes and doing things differently in future. You have paid for your mistakes. You have carried this pain for a lifetime. That has been a prison sentence. You've done your time. If you want to make amends, then you do that by letting this go, learning from it, and using what you learn to give something back to the world. Are you ready to do that?"

He might say "I need to apologise to Mark".

If that happens, I just bring Mark into the visualisation and let him say sorry to Mark. Mark doesn't get to say whether my younger self spends the rest of his lifetime punishing himself. That's not Mark's call. My younger self is sorry to Mark, and he expresses this sincerely. If Mark forgives him that's a bonus, but ultimately my younger self and I get to decide how this story ends. All he can do is offer his sincere apology. It's all he's got. If my younger self needs any help here, that's what I'm going to tell him. "You've said you're sorry. What Mark does with that is up to him now. You've done all you can. All that matters now is that you let it go."

Now I have to listen for his response. What does the feeling do now?

The outcome we are hoping for here, is that I'll experience a profound shift. I'll know that he's received the message. If I have a visual representation of him in my mind, I will see him brighten up and stand up straight. Maybe I'll just receive a sense that I feel less burdened. If necessary, I'll continue to dialogue with him. He may have further questions. At some point, I am hoping that I will see him shift away from feeling unforgivable, into an acknowledgement that it's time to let it go now.

The act of witnessing those long-held feelings, coupled with compassion and re-explaining the meaning of that event will usually be enough for him to see himself differently. His image of himself as an unforgivable monster, deserving of endless punishment, will be transformed into a recognition of a self who is learning to be a better person. Just as with the previous exercise, if you are able to successfully dialogue to this point of transformation, you can expect that you will experience a permanent transformation in the way that you feel about yourself.

You can again test the change by saying the following statement.

"I have forgiven myself for bullying Mark at school". (Obviously, you will replace "Mark at school" with whatever you happen to be working on).

Notice how that feels now. If you get a neutral or positive feeling in your body when you speak those words, you can take it that this has been accepted at the unconscious level. That is a signal that this work is complete.

If, after running this process, you find that there is still resistance to your message, and you feel that this is important work to do for your ongoing well-being, then I have to recommend meeting with a therapist. A therapist should be able to help you work through any persistent resistances.

Regardless of the immediate outcome, for now, it's time to close the session. Thank your younger self for meeting with you. Let him know that you consider him forgivable, and tell him that you have his back from hereon in, before returning to your waking state of consciousness. Whatever the outcome, you have extended caring and compassion to yourself at the deepest level. This is never a bad thing.

In the above example, my current adult self has provided my younger self with new understanding which my younger self can use to recognise that he is forgivable. I have acted as a friend and mentor towards him.

Put that example in its own box for a moment because we're now going to take a look at a different situation.

When it comes to forgiving yourself for something you may have done to yourself (as opposed to someone else), the format is similar.

Let's suppose that I cheated on the love of my life, and she's now married to someone else. I hate myself every single day for that mistake. I haven't had a relationship in ten years. Unconsciously, I don't trust myself, and I am determined to punish myself with loneliness in some twisted effort to make amends. Clearly, I am at war with myself on this.

I close my eyes and settle in. I say,

"I have forgiven myself for ruining my relationship with Lisa".

Strong feelings will emerge as my inner lie-detector tells me that I just spoke garbage. The truth is, that I have feelings of deep pain, anger and loss. I sit with them. I acknowledge them deeply, and here, just as in the previous example, I really want to connect with how deeply I regret what has happened. With that connection, I speak with every bit of sincerity I have, to whatever "part" of myself is carrying that pain. I say:-

"I know that you have found it really hard to forgive me for my mistakes. I am truly, deeply, sorry. I know I screwed up royally, and I know that it has had a disastrous effect on you. I am truly...truly...sorry".

If you are really feeling this as you speak it, then you will get your message across. I wait, and watch, for his response. If necessary, I dialogue with him. I may explain, as I did in the last example, that there is nothing to be gained by my continued punishment. I may ask him directly for his forgiveness. What matters is that I will speak from my heart. This is not grovelling to myself. This is an expression of my genuine regret. It is an act of real humility. I am humbling myself to him, and doing so willingly. He does not have to forgive me. He may need more time. As with the apology to Mark, this is all I've got. What matters is that I've done the decent thing. That carries real weight. Maybe this will **begin** a process of self-forgiveness?

In addition to saying that I'm sorry for what might have been done in the past, it may be extremely important to offer some reassurances that the same thing will not happen again. If I can say with my hand on my heart "I promise that I will **never** cheat on a loved one again", then I should offer that to him as a sacred vow. If I do this though, I'd better make sure I don't break it. Restoring trust once is difficult enough. If you make promises you don't keep, don't be surprised if your deeper self is less willing to forgive you in future.

It's much better then, if I cannot give any guarantees, to say so, and then give what I can. This shouldn't be weak and watery. How would you feel if someone gave you some half-baked reassurances? A sincere assurance without guarantees might sound like this: -

"I am sincerely sorry. I cannot give you a cast iron guarantee that I won't screw up **ever** again in some way but I do promise you from the very bottom of my heart that I have every intention of not letting you down in this way ever again. I will do everything which is within my control to get it right from this point forwards."

As long as that really is your pure intention, and you genuinely do have regret, there's no reason why that should not be acceptable grounds for self-forgiveness to begin or complete. We are human. We do make mistakes, often more than once. Our best will have to be good enough. If you're not being honest with yourself though, and think this will get you off the hook so that you can misbehave again, you'll be in for a rough ride. Deceiving oneself on matters of great importance is not a wise move. Nothing is hidden. We risk falling out of trust with ourselves in a damaging way. The rule is:-

Don't offer what you can't deliver.

If you're honest with yourself though, that alone can be grounds for reconciliation, even if you can't currently offer much more than an apology. It's really no different from any other relationship. If you're confused in any way on what to offer, just imagine how you might feel if someone asked for your forgiveness on a matter. What would you want to hear from them? Whatever that is, it is the same thing you want to hear from yourself.

Good luck! I hope this is super powerful healing work for you. Remember, your heart is in the right place, but you're human, and you've made mistakes. You are working to be a better person. You may have doubts. That's okay. You give what you can for now. Stay with that theme, and you shouldn't go too far wrong. If your situation is complex, some professional assistance with a therapist may be advisable. Sometimes these things need a bit of unpicking, but keeping it simple, a heartfelt apology to your deepest self will often make a huge difference to how you feel towards yourself.

Chapter Nineteen - Recovering Your Personal Power

Earlier on in the book, I spoke at length about the question of who you were before you got your heart broken – your original innocence. Remember, this is not only who you were, but who you really are, in your wholeness. I've also discussed with you the notion that your essential innocence remains a part of your being, even if you have experienced significant wounding, or lacked the positive experience in life to connect with your full potential.

What I haven't discussed with you yet is the possibility that some of your essential innocence may be out of your reach because you may have given some part of yourself away, or had a part of yourself taken from you under duress. Instead of thinking of this proposal too literally, consider it as an analogy. You'll be familiar with the often quoted *"when he went away...he took a piece of me with him."* These are allusions to this theme of fragmentation, and we can all relate in some way.

In addition to losing something of yourself to someone else, you may also be unwittingly carrying someone else's psychological "stuff". This can occur as an ongoing relationship dynamic, or in the form of a historic event which has left you feeling less than whole and deeply burdened ever since it happened.

Let's begin by exploring what this means in current situations. We can become the unwitting carriers of other peoples' "baggage" because we have **agreed,** at an unconscious level, to carry their burden for them. An example of this might be a friend who continually tells you all their bad news and only ever moans and groans when you visit them. You're a super nice person so you try to be a good friend. You leave their house feeling terrible, and they thank you for coming around and tell you how much better they feel now.

Those who drain you may be in some way "plugging in" to you. You can think of this as an energetic matter if that's your chosen model, or you can think of it psychologically. The energetic (symbolic) perspective would require you to imagine that this person is somehow invisibly siphoning your energy from you through a vulnerable place in your psyche – psychic vampirism, if you will. The psychological (clinical) explanation would be that this person exhausts you because their behaviours triggers stress responses in your body, or they insist that you bring an unnatural level of concentration and attention to them which makes you feel depleted.

At some level, they are exerting invisible control over you, or put another way, you are experiencing powerlessness in their presence. They are **taking** from you in the sense that they are demanding a level of attention or acquiescence which you'd prefer not to give, and they are also **dumping** on you when they burden you with their negativity or emotional baggage. You are now carrying their stuff. This can happen chronically too, so that we end up feeling like we are responsible for other people's lives because they refuse to be responsible for their own. These people are often referred to as energetic vampires because they drain you of any good feelings, and give you little or nothing back in return.

Whether there really is a transfer of energy from you to them or from them to you is questionable and debatable. In the end it doesn't really matter. The point is, that we experience it **as if** it were the case, and we need to work with this at the narrative level because the language that the unconscious mind uses, which is where all of this phenomenon is taking place, is that of **symbol and narrative.**

If we begin by thinking about current situations, we can ask: - Are there people in your life who drain you when you spend time with them? Do you feel disempowered around particular individuals?

If you can identify people who drain you, take it as a given that there is an imbalance of power within the relationship. In this chapter, we are going to work on restoring balance so that you are no longer at their mercy.

In addition to current imbalances of power in relationships, we also know that there are events which have left us feeling disempowered long after the situation or person is history to us. What might that be about?

Let's take for example an abusive parent. Maybe the parent constantly told the child that their estranged father was a loser. What has that parent "dumped" on their child? That's a case of the mother dumping her anger towards her ex-husband on the child. Any other more deliberate physical or emotional abuse is a form of dumping too. It's not always outright abuse either. It can be subtle, taking the form of undermining comments hidden behind a veneer of joviality and friendliness. There goes the saying "many a true word spoken in jest".

All of these behaviours are a lack of emotional ownership and responsibility on the part of the parent, which calls for the child to bear or share the weight. That's dumping. At some level, that child walks away from that situation with the weight of the world on his or her shoulders. Unless that weight is rejected, it might remain in place indefinitely.

The inverse, and usually co-existing form of this, is when the parent robs a child of their safety, confidence, trust, or well-being. Instead of dumping, now they are "taking" something from the child. A parent who tells their child that they will never amount to anything is stealing that child's sense of self-confidence. A sexual abuser will potentially rob a child of their innocence. They'll probably dump their own shame on them at the same time. We know that children often think that it's their fault that they were abused. A violent and unpredictable parent will rob a child of his or her sense of safety in the world. Again, unless that "power" is recovered, it may remain absent.

A self-image which is anything other than loveable and valuable, has in part, been "given" to us at some level.

When a positive self-image is unavailable, it's possible that something has been "taken" from us, somewhere down the line.

At a highly symbolic level, the survivors of these terrible situations may experience themselves as diminished. A piece of their soul may feel as though it is missing, and they may feel like they are carrying something heavy, without any conscious understanding of why life seems so exhausting. The worst damage is done to people during childhood because not only are we highly impressionable as children, but we also don't have enough experience in life to recognise that what is being done to us is not okay or normal, and fail to rebuff it adequately. That's deep programming, and unpicking that in later life is difficult.

For explanation's sake, I've used some extremely serious subjects here. I don't want to give the impression that the method I'm about to present to you is going to be sufficient or suitable for matters such as childhood sexual abuse. You know what I'm going to say, right? Get professional help. Seriously. Don't carry that on your own. It may be too big to work through alone, so don't try. Nonetheless, it's still worth explaining these processes because they'll highlight that the work is worth doing. For those without devastating trauma, you might find what follows truly liberating.

If you experience significant disempowerment in life, then there is something you need to know quite urgently.

At some level, you are giving/have given people <u>permission</u> to treat you in a way that you do not wish to be treated.

If the loss or burden is historic, then it means that you **once** gave someone permission to dump on you and/or take from you. If you're still feeling disempowered, then it's a firm bet that there's still an imbalance being played out within your psyche. It will probably be the case that you feel disempowered around people or situations which resemble the original trauma. The "story" is that you can't handle people or situations which look like that.

Whether it's current or historical, matters little. The unconscious mind sees little difference between past, present, and future, or real and imagined. The abusive power dynamic is established at some point, and that's the way it stays until we take steps to formally address the matter and do something about it.

What I want to highlight here then is that **permission can be revoked at any time.**

Stop here. Take a moment to really understand what I just said. <u>Permission can be taken back</u>. You are allowed to change your mind. I said earlier that sometimes we unconsciously agree to give something of ourselves away, or carry someone else's burden because we are under duress. It is very often the case that a situation occurs which is so tricky to navigate, that we see no other option than to sacrifice something of ourselves in order to survive, or make it right. That in itself is sometimes unavoidable, and no mistake has been made. The problem is, that the rules which are set at that particular moment in history will remain in operation going forwards because they simply become the normalised way of doing business in that relationship, or relationships of a similar nature.

Relationships, incidentally, as far as the unconscious mind is concerned, exist in a timeless vacuum. It's been forty years since Miss Jackson, our second-year primary school teacher struck fear into the hearts of her pupils, but we all still shudder at the mention of her name. We, the utterly powerless seven-year olds were only ever a moment away from some terrible fate or other (I forget now!) She was ferocious. My mind cares little for the fact that she would hold no actual power over me today were she here. The relationship is sealed in time as one in which I hold no power, and my mind presents this as an immutable fact.

So...let's get your power back, shall we?

Here's a few words about what the exercise intends to achieve, and then we'll learn how to do it. The usual disclaimer applies.

Primarily, this exercise is intended to work at a number of levels. The first of these, and perhaps the most important, is that it works at the level of the **narrative** which you carry within you. The past is gone, done, finished. The **story** of your disempowerment as a result of that past, remains, frozen in time, and that means that your subconscious mind is still operating from those rules. We want to change that. In a way, the reason those rules have remained in place is because you have never formally taken your power back and/or revoked permission, most probably because you've never really considered it from this perspective before. So, at one level this is about taking your power back (literally, as we'll see in a moment) and also revoking all and any permissions you may have given at any time, either consciously, unconsciously, or under duress.

Beyond this, we also have an opportunity here to benefit from a little self-hypnosis style visualisation work. Thus, we are employing symbol and narrative, which as I mentioned earlier, are prime languages for the unconscious mind, and often, a superior healer.

As with all of these exercises provided here, you are invited to spend a few minutes moving into a quiet focussed state of awareness before you begin.

Then, when you're quiet and focussed, with your eyes closed, you imagine a figure eight like the one shown here. You place yourself in the "You" circle, and you place the person you feel disempowered around in the opposite circle ("Them"). They can be a current figure or a historical one. If they are deceased that doesn't make any difference. This isn't really about them. It's about you and your internal story. The rules are that the person in the opposite circle cannot come into your circle, so your circle remains a safe space. There is nothing else in either circle. You imagine the other person standing still.

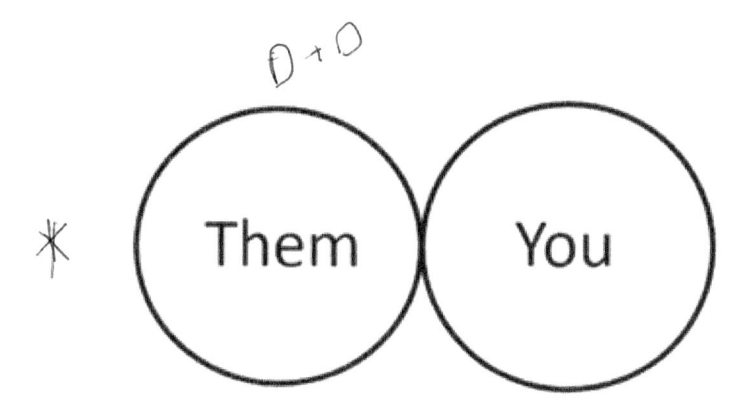

(Them)(You)

Begin by taking a look at them in this highly neutral space. What do you see? How do they look to you? Are they huge and menacing, or in this neutral space, are they plain and ordinary? Spend a few moments allowing yourself to just look at them. You may gain some insight about them which you've never seen in day to day life before. Without the trappings of their wealth or power, maybe they are rather lonely, or sad, or afraid? Whatever you see is fine. Just note it. You can feel safe. They can't come into your space. Should you feel alarmed at any point, you can end the exercise if you wish, but generally this is an exercise which is extremely easy to do, and shouldn't cause any fear.

Now, you're going to trust your gut here. Focus on your feeling body (ie just be present in your body and notice what you feel inside), and then speak the following words out loud: -

"What am I carrying which belongs to this person?"

[handwritten annotations: dirty jokes, anger, hate, lust, murder]

The intention here, is to identify anything which this person may have dumped on you, or that you have agreed to shoulder on their behalf (sometimes unknowingly). Now, pay attention to your body and feelings. What comes up?

At this point, it's quite usual for somebody to say that they have become aware of a weight on the chest, or a sensation in the belly. Whatever appears, take your attention to it and notice whether it has a shape, a colour, or a texture. Is it light or heavy, small or large? Any sensory impressions you can identify will help to bring the "object" into clearer focus, but you know, it really doesn't matter if it's just vague. The important thing is to locate where you have been holding that tension in your body. Just as in the earlier exercises, speaking the question will activate your unconscious awareness, and your (feeling) body will reveal the relevant content to you.

In some instances, people will report a specific object. They might say that it's like a lead weight on the chest, a dagger through the heart, a dull blackness in the belly, or it may be an object which has personal significance to you such as a book, a ring, or some other symbol. Trust what you sense. Your unconscious mind is using the language which is appropriate to you personally in how it presents this material. It might make logical sense, or it might not. Don't analyse it (you can wonder later). Just stay focussed.

It's possible that you will receive a neutral response in your body. If that happens, it means one of two things. Either you genuinely are not carrying anything which belongs to that person. If that's the case, there's nothing more to do in this part of the exercise. Make a mental note that you're not carrying a burden relating to this person and trust that it's true. Your unconscious mind will let you know if there's something to do here.

Or, it means that your unconscious mind simply isn't going to play ball today. You'll have to figure out which it is. You should have a pretty clear sense of "there's nothing", if that is the case. Otherwise, just try the exercise another day if you wish. We can definitely get different results on different days, so don't sweat on it. There's no failure here, only feedback.

Assuming you have successfully located the negativity, tension, symbol, poor self-image, or emotional baggage which this person dumped on you, we are now going to return that material to them. Don't feel bad about doing this. You are not being cruel. You must understand that you are doing them a favour. They cannot heal their wounding if they are not in possession of it. You've got your own stuff to deal with. This is theirs, and it has no business being in your body. What they choose to do with it once you have returned it to them is entirely up to them. They can heal it if they wish. If they choose not to, then that is not on you. We all play by the same rules. You're doing the right thing by working on you. Be very clear that returning to it to them is exactly what needs to happen.

Walk up to the centre of the figure eight where the two circles meet. Holding your mind steady, you imagine reaching into your body and removing the offending material so that you are now holding it in your hands, in front of you. Now, gently drop it into the circle opposite you and as you do so, make the following statement, out loud:-

"This X (state what it is – tension, hatred, bitterness, anger, poor self-image, sadness, belief etc) does not belong to me. It is yours. I cannot heal this for you. You must do it yourself. I refuse to carry this on your behalf any longer. I revoke all and any permissions I have ever given, consciously or unconsciously, for you to have me carry your stuff. From this point forwards I will not carry this for you anymore".

I cannot stress strongly enough how important it is that you say these words with complete conviction. You need to really mean business. It's not a request. It's a statement of fact. You do not require their permission. That's the whole point. There is no discussion to be had. You are not asking. You are telling. This is deeply symbolic and powerful. Bring gravitas to this moment. Step into your power and feel your autonomy.

Once you have released the burden back to its rightful owner, step back into the centre of your own circle and take a moment to focus on the area where you were holding that weight. How does it feel now? Is it different? Notice any change.

Now ask again, "Am I holding or carrying anything else which belongs to this person?"

If another tension, shape, sensation, or symbol arises, simply repeat the process. Continue then, for as many rounds as is necessary, until you receive a fully neutral response in your body when you ask the "Am I holding anything…?" question. You'll know when it's clear. There will simply be no response, or a clear "no" signal. Your unconscious mind will register this. It will "update" your internal narrative accordingly. The story that you are subservient to this individual will no longer exist. As far as your unconscious mind is concerned, there has been another meeting which has re-written the rules.

We are halfway done. Next, we want to recover anything which has been taken from you. We open this part of the work with the following question: -

"Does this person have anything which rightfully belongs to me?"

Speak it out loud, and pay attention to what your body/mind tells you. Again, trust your gut. You'll know. Did this person take your innocence, your power, your confidence, your happiness, your sex drive, or your self-worth?

When you know what they've got of yours, remaining in the centre of your circle (remember it's a protected space), you now simply demand (speaking out loud) that it be returned to you immediately. Say it with authority. It's not a request. It's an absolute demand. Take it as a rule of dynamics that nobody is permitted to hold anything which belongs to you unless you give them permission to do so. You can, again state, that if you ever gave permission for them to take anything from you, or whether you ever gave them something of yourself, that you are now revoking those permissions fully and permanently.

As a general rule, surprisingly, the person in the other circle will cough it up pretty quickly. Tell them to drop it into your circle (this is allowed). You can then walk over and pick it up, whatever it is. It may be an object, or it may be non-distinct. It doesn't matter. Whatever it looks like, just pick it up and hold it in your hands in front of you for a moment.

Just as you meant business when you returned what had been dumped on you, it's equally important that you engage your determination, and imagination, as fully as possible in the next moment too. Bring your hands to your chest and imagine the object/quality/power etc melting, dissolving, into your body again. As the object enters your chest, breathe in deeply and feel that lost part of yourself reuniting with your entire being as it returns home to you. Imagine that quality flowing to every part of your being with every pump of your heart.

If you recovered your "confidence" from that person, then imagine how it **feels** to have that "I can do this" feeling returning to your body. If you recovered your "happiness", then feel that natural state of joy pouring through your system. Remember how natural it is. Notice that you don't have to pretend it or manufacture it. It just is. Stay with this. Don't be in a hurry to close the exercise. Take a few moments to luxuriate in the experience of recovering such a precious part of your well-being. Welcome it home, and feel into your new sense of fullness.

When you're ready, imagine the circles separating, and visualise the "them" circle disappearing into the distance, returning that person to their own time and space. Take a moment to see yourself "at cause" in your own circle. "At cause" is a way of saying "no longer under the effect" of that person. Your business is complete. You have disentangled yourself from their influence. All of this is updating your internal narrative.

Then, gently, return to your ordinary state of waking awareness, feeling good, and when you are ready, allow your eyes to open. Take a few moments before going back to your busy-ness, to contemplate the meaning and power of the exercise you just did. Make a mental note of any empowered feelings you now have, and make a commitment to operate with that spirit, from this point forwards. Hopefully you will really **feel** the difference. When it comes to putting this stuff into practice in the real world, that sense of strength is what's going to make it possible.

CHAPTER TWENTY – WHO'S GOT YOUR BACK?

"Who's got your back?" was going to be the title for this book. I had to re-think this, reluctantly, because that title just wasn't clear enough as a description of the book's contents, and wouldn't be found by people searching for help on this subject.

The spirit of that title though, remains central to what this book is ultimately about. Others may have your back in all sorts of ways, but as human beings, we all have to cope with experiences which are intensely private. Our grief, our pain, our anxiety, our depression, our doubts, our weaknesses, and our failures. Others can walk beside us, but only we ourselves can walk in our shoes.

Kindness from others has value but internal suffering can make us feel extremely isolated. In extreme states of crisis, shock, grief, depression, or anxiety, we can feel dissociated from the world, so that everything seems to exist on the other side of a thick pane of glass. People are speaking to us but they're like apparitions which we cannot touch or properly connect with. When we are in such private hells, the counsel of others, while well meaning, can be difficult to receive. We know that nobody can really know what we are going through, and no matter how understanding they may seem, our suffering is still ultimately private. We alone will carry it, and we alone will ultimately heal it.

> **There is really only one person who can fully know what you're going through...and that is you.** +Jesus + H S

Even if we are able to receive the empathy and compassion offered by loved ones, nobody has time to hold our hand for twenty-four hours a day. Your suffering doesn't end when your partner leaves for work.

Who then is better placed to be fully present and supportive in such difficult moments in life than <u>you</u>?

That makes the relationship that you have with yourself the single most important relationship you can possibly have. If you don't have that one in good shape, then life's worst moments are going to be extraordinarily lonely at best, and tortured at worst, no matter how much your mum or your spouse loves you. Sometimes, we simply can't be reached by anyone on the outside of ourselves. If we're in self-punishment mode alongside the misery of difficult circumstances, then we're really in a bad place. That's reason number one that <u>self-love is an imperative component of well-being generally, and almost indispensable if we're in need of healing.</u>

There is, however, an equally pressing reason to ensure that we've got our inner-relationship with ourselves in order. This is a challenging world. It's a world of anxiety, hostility, division, competition, scarcity, exploitation, disagreement, injustice, and woundedness, to name only a few of the regular disturbances we will face. It feels a bit gloomy to write those words but if the perspective seems unnecessarily negative, consider for a moment whether you've personally escaped being on the receiving end of any of the above? The chances are you've experienced them all and a whole bunch more besides.

These challenges usually don't consume our entire lives but they are an ever-present threat for most of us, and one of the goals here is to help people to reduce their anxiety levels. Our anxiety levels are intrinsically linked to how threatened we feel at any given moment. The more threatened we feel, the more anxious we become. We feel threatened when we don't feel that we have the resources available to protect ourselves, or a "reason" to do so. There is no reason to protect something dear to us more powerful than that we have love for it.

> **Self-love isn't just about being nice to yourself. True self-love needs to include the ferocious protective instinct that a parent has for their child.**
>
> *tiger*

In other words, we need to be able to stick up for ourselves. That doesn't mean that we need to live defensively. That's a recipe for being an angry human being who doesn't trust anyone. It means that we need to know that we have the necessary strength, skill, and spirit, available to protect ourselves should we **need** to do so. True power doesn't walk around with its chest puffed out. It's generally quiet and humble.

Many parents will recognise the feeling that they would gladly lay down their own lives to protect their offspring. True love is full of fight when it needs to be. We will fight for the things that matter to us. The idea that love is some kind of soft touch is a complete misunderstanding of what love actually is. Love is caring and valuing, and if that means that there needs to be a fight in order to protect the object of our love, then so be it. The ultimate expression of deep self-love, as it is with a parent and child, is a willingness to die, if necessary, to protect the integrity of the self.

These are strong words, and terribly melodramatic. We hope, of course, that nothing so drastic will be required, and that we'll die at a ripe old age with peace in our hearts, happiness for a life well lived, and surrounded by loved ones. What I'm attempting to communicate here though is a **spirit** of commitment towards oneself which is **completely reliable** to the (hopefully avoidable) bitter end.

A metaphorical image comes to mind. As I go about my daily business interacting with the world, it's as if there are two of me. Typically, I see myself as an adult, and I see my second self, my friend, as a child (though it doesn't have to be a child). For me, that child represents everything which is pure and innocent, fragile and wide open within me. He walks next to me. He doesn't fear judgement. He is playful, light, curious, excitable, friendly, generous, welcoming, caring, trusting, spontaneous, and adventurous. As I go about my business, he's there, quietly reminding me how to live lightly, be kinder, remember what's truly important, and to have a little fun each day. Many of the people I interact with have a friend by their side too. We have a similar understanding of the world, and there's an unspoken agreement that we'll treat each other with kindness because it's a brighter world when we do so. I recognise that hearts are fragile, and they do too. We do our best to be gentle with each other.

One day, another human who has no child by his side walks toward me. I reach out to my side and quickly pull the boy in so that he now stands behind me. My sixth sense has been triggered. *Where's this guy's friend?* I've met people without friends by their side before. They can be dangerous. They have less to lose. Sometimes they are on the warpath. My gut tells me to beware of the unloved.

This doesn't imply that all wounded people are hostile but it is fair to say that people who are at peace in themselves tend to be less threatening than those who are not. I'm not fixing for a fight. Neither am I expecting every person or situation I encounter to be a danger to me. It's merely a precautionary measure. Whatever comes from our interaction, and there's every reason to expect that it will be perfectly amicable, there's no way that I'm going to let him hurt my inner-human. In practice, this is a deep inner certainty that I'd rather die than allow my inner-human to be bullied or abused. I feel no fear about this. I'm prepared to do whatever is necessary to protect him. It's absolutely what must be done.

It sounds dramatic, I know, to say that I would "die" for him, but it really isn't about expecting a catastrophe. It's a "whatever it takes" position. Our deepest selves want to know that we won't quit on them when the going gets tough. Fairweather friends need not apply. Courage is required.

How did I get there? Well, it's simple really. I was given a second chance. Rarely do we understand how much something means to us, until we lose it. I became deeply estranged from myself as a result of trauma, anxiety, and depression in my twenties, and I learned that being alone inside is excruciatingly painful. Being at war with yourself is worse still. As I rebuilt my relationship with myself, I learned that inner-trust is hard earned. It involves making some sacrifices, and when you work hard for something so important you tend to value it enormously. Value, you will remember, is another word for love. I automatically developed some fierce protectiveness towards my inner-human. I can't live a good life without him. We need each other, and if he can't count on me when it really matters, it leaves room for ongoing existential anxiety. Beyond the mental noise that any human brain produces, he knows that I've got his back.

When this feeling of inner-certainty that you'll do whatever you need to do to self-protect is present, our anxiety naturally reduces. We will not then spend our lives in a constant state of "what if?". "What if?" becomes irrelevant. It doesn't matter what happens. **You've** got your back!

Chapter Twenty One – Dealing With Bullies

If I was in the business of carrying shame around, I have a few memories I could do without. Recently, I reconnected with an old schoolfriend on social media, and we started to have some in-depth discussions. Just to make sure everything was tidy between us, I said, "I hope I was always nice to you at school? I wasn't ever horrible, was I?"

"Well, it's funny you should ask." she said.

She went on to tell me a story. We were about six years old. She and I were in class, and somehow, she managed to spill yellow paint on my cardigan. Evidently, I couldn't let it go. Apparently, I then chased her across the field at lunch time and thumped her. She said she was running, and in her head, she had the thought, "I can't believe it. John Crawford is chasing me!" Not in a good way either. I have absolutely no memory of this. I was mortified. I have apologised profusely. She tells me I'm forgiven. I believe her.

Here's another public post I wrote a couple of years ago which tells of a couple of my life lessons from a tender age: -

Hello. Today's musings: - As a hypnotherapist, I know how important significant events are in shaping who we become. Today, I want to share two important memories, both of which taught me that being kind in life is the best way to go, but both from entirely different angles. Those early teenage years are a confusing time at best, as we try to figure out who we are and develop a persona that works. I'm quite ashamed of this memory, but I'm pleased it happened.

I was at the local summer carnival. I passed another boy who went to my school, who for some reason, I had decided I didn't want to be associated with. As we passed, he waved and said Hi. I forget exactly what I said, but I was trying to be the big "I am", and it was something along the lines of "Don't talk to me". He instantly launched at me with a flurry of punches, and within moments I had a cut swollen lip and blood pumping all over my nice new white jacket. I had a humiliating bus journey home, covered in blood. But it wasn't my lip that hurt the most, or my pride (though that was bruised too!) What hurt the most was looking at the fact that I totally deserved it. There was no getting away from it. I just felt really ashamed of myself for being such a jerk!

The second memory is thankfully much sweeter. I grew up in the '70's, and the main forms of entertainment in my primary school were football, marbles, and conkers. I was crazy about my marble collection. I literally knew every single marble intimately, and they were, to me, the most precious objects in existence. We played for keeps. One day I took a risk, and agreed to play one of my favourite marbles against an older boy. I was about seven years old. The odds were in my favour, since his marble was much more ordinary, which meant he'd have to hit mine three times more to win. I lost! As I handed over "my precious", I burst into tears. I was distraught. Seeing how upset I was, he handed the marble back to me. He wrote his win off, and let me keep my marble. My heart swelled with gratitude. He might as well have released me from a life imprisonment. I was so relieved. This boy went on to be the best man at my wedding, and is one of my closest friends to this day. I recounted the story to him when we were adults, and he had no memory of it whatsoever, but for me, it had been life changing. I had learned what receiving real kindness felt like that day, and I remember resolving to be more like that. A few years ago, he sent me a big bag of the most beautiful marbles in the post, completely out of the blue. What a gesture!

Instant karma is a great teacher, but acts of kindness go even deeper! Have a great day x (End)

Bullying has been a big theme in my life. When I was training as a hypnotherapist, I undertook a course of analytical hypnotherapy as a patient, in order to fully understand the process as a recipient. I found it utterly fascinating, and I've written elsewhere about some of the unusual experiences I had during that period. A central theme which emerged though, was bullying. In particular, two pivotal memories stood out.

One involved me standing up for a black girl who was being bullied for her skin colour by the scariest bully in the school. I could have received a beating myself but I was so incensed, that I did it anyway, and somehow escaped injury. I was five years old. I know that because it happened in my very first classroom.

In another, a boy of Turkish origin was being bullied, also for skin colour. I think they were kicking him, and he was trying to get away. He was my friend. He held himself with great dignity. There was something very graceful and gentle about him, but he was strong. I'd never seen him cry. On this particular day though, he just broke. He burst into tears, and I remember my heart absolutely breaking for him. It was such a shock to see my beautiful graceful friend lose his poise. There was something so brutal and pointless about taking something so beautiful, and smashing it. It really affected me. I comforted him after the bullies left, and he composed himself, but I felt heartbroken for him for a long time afterwards. I think I witnessed the actual moment that his innocence was taken from him. It still makes me tearful to think of it now.

Only a few years ago now, I was in the driveway to my house, and I heard shouting from the top of the road. A young boy from the local school was walking down the street begging another boy to return his scooter to him. He was crying. It was evident that a group of other boys had stolen it from him. One of the boys from the offending group said, "Go on, give him back his scooter". At this point, the thief relented and went to return it to him but the scooter owner seemed to suddenly realise that the scooter wasn't the point. He turned away and said "keep the f*****g scooter". I was ready to intervene but now they were chasing him to return the scooter as he walked away, so I wasn't needed.

I turned, went back into my house, and immediately sobbed. Not just a tear on the cheek but great big belly-shaking sobs. It really triggered something deeply sad within me.

It's hardly surprising. As a child I lived in fear. I've had my ribs broken in a bullying beating I received. I've been held at knifepoint, and I've been stalked and threatened. I'm sure there are tens of incidents which have been mercifully repressed or erased from my memories. It was rough where I grew up. One particularly unhinged young lad used to terrify me. He was not just a loudmouth. In fact, he was quiet, and that was what made him truly sinister. He oozed evil. One day, when I was walking home from school alone, he accosted me on a quiet street and told me he was going to kill me. He was kicking and punching me to get a reaction. I had done absolutely nothing to provoke him. I just happened to be there. I think he was seriously considering killing me, and there was something about him that made me know that it wasn't bluster. It was chilling. I changed my route home and carefully timed my exit from school to avoid ever being caught alone by him again.

I'm sure we all have our own stories.

Bullying is a serious problem. It can be a primary cause of mental illness. It can cause people to take their own lives, and it can permanently rob people of their innocence and self-worth in a single moment. What a tragedy. And, for what?

I'm afraid I don't have all the answers for you on this one. Some bullies are truly dangerous. Most bullies though are wounded, cowardly souls, who get off on picking on the vulnerable, usually because they feel so wretched themselves. It's no secret that most people who abuse others are recipients of abuse themselves, sadly.

What I do want to offer though is a little bit of insight into the psychology of bullies so that you can be better placed to know what the right thing to do is when you meet one. I'm going to do this by sharing a few stories with you.

I'll start with one of my own.

It was my first year in high school. I was eleven years old, and about four feet tall. For some reason, one of the bullies from two years above me had decided to put me on his target list. There were months of minor bullying - name calling and ear flicking, that sort of thing. One day we passed on the stairs, and he pushed me and flicked my face. I just lost it. I took a swing and completely missed. At this point, I thought I was dead. At the age of thirteen, he was pretty much a fully-grown man, physically speaking. He stood at about five foot-ten. He literally took me by the back of my jacket (probably with one hand) and hung me up in the air. His mates were laughing hysterically, and then one of them said, "Ah...leave him alone...he's only little". He then put me down and we all went about our business. For the rest of my school life, he was always really nice to me and I think he even may have defended me once or twice. I'd had no chance of winning that battle but I had earned his respect, and I eventually came to think of him as quite a nice guy.

Here's another: -

A friend of mine owns a small hotel in Spain. She has fought tooth and nail to make it work, for eight long years, and is now finally in the black. We were speaking recently and she was telling us about how she has her boundaries frequently tested, as a hotel owner, by people who have unreasonable demands. She had encountered just such a customer recently who had turned nasty when she told him he couldn't overstay in his room, as it was booked to another customer. A short campaign of menace was then unleashed upon her personally, which culminated, after a period of days, in her walking down the street and noticing that he was coming towards her. She thought about diverting but something in her just said "No". She carried on until they were close enough that he was able to deliver a threat to her, and then she just snapped. She said that she felt the full weight of her eight years of struggle rise up in her, and she was blasted if she was going to let anyone threaten all that she'd worked so hard to build.

She strode up to him and confronted him face on.

"Okay. What are you going to do? Are you going to kill me?! Are you?! Well you better get it done then because I'm not going to be intimidated by you!"

He backed down, and the campaign of menace ended. She's never seen him since. We call her "Hotel Momma". I love her. She's inspiring.

This last story came to me from a particularly lovely reader who I've been chatting with. We were talking about nastiness and kindness, and she happened to email me with this story. She's kindly allowed me to include it here: -

One year when I was about thirteen, I let a much larger and taller girl than me call me names, push me around, and get up in my face and threaten me.

*I put up with a lot, usually in front of an audience of our peers. Then, one day, I happened to run into her at my family farm, where her friend's family had been hired to help discourage trespassers and thieves. It was just her and me on my land, crossing paths, going to different destinations. She started in with her "smack talk", shoving me, and something inside just clicked. All of a sudden, I was shoving her, up in her face growling, "go ahead and beat me up if that's what your intent is, but know this, I'll be damned if you're going to come onto **my** property, and **my** farm, and think that you can push **me** around. So, go ahead and take your best shot, because I may be smaller than you, and I may get my butt kicked, but I'm going to hurt you so badly that you're going to know that you've been in a fight, because I'm done with putting up with your crap!" She jumped back with a surprised expression on her face. She was about a foot taller than me, and probably twice as heavy, since I was a skinny girl of average height. I was ready to fight her if that was going to get her to finally leave me alone. She looked at me shame-faced, backed up, apologized, and went away to find her friend. I don't think that anyone had ever stood up to her before, so she ruled at school through intimidation.*

*After that day, and right up until the end of high school, she was polite towards me, treated me nicely, as though we were the best of friends. She said "hello" whenever she saw me, even from across the parking lot, and she even smiled kindly and called me by my real name, instead of calling me foul names. She even made all of her previously mean friends, who'd backed her and hung out with her, treat me nicely as well! I was completely surprised by the difference between us then, as opposed to how she had always treated me before. Sometimes, the only way to stop a bully is by being prepared to be beaten up, and offering to fight them - stand up for yourself, instead of being polite and nice in the face of adversity. Unsurprisingly, I wouldn't exactly say that we were true friends afterwards, but I'd gained her respect, and as a result, she was nice to almost everyone else afterwards as well. Her whole attitude towards everyone else changed, and she became **nice**! And, as a result, everyone was nice to her and her friends. That resulted from one of my "tea kettle" moments! If I hadn't blown my top, she would've continued to torment me, and dozens of people who were like me, forever! So that segment of my life has a happy ending to a bad start.*

I found this a beautiful read, and what particularly stands out for me, is how the bully changed her ways and learned that people would be nice to her if she was nice to them. Isn't that just about the whole message, right there? Like I said, I don't really think most people are bad. They just need a little help getting on the right track. It seems, in this case, that this act of courage did the job. The fellow who clobbered me for being a jerk did me a massive favour. It was the first and last time I ever tried to bully anyone. Standing up to a bully might be more than only a service to yourself. It might do them a favour too.

I think the stories speak for themselves. Obviously, the message here isn't that you should start having physical confrontations with people. The message is that bullies generally don't bully people who stand up for themselves. In just a short while, we'll be exploring how to own your voice and use it to express your power. In addition, let's remember that there are laws and institutional systems available to deal with bullies. If things are that bad for you, use them. Otherwise, use your voice. It has enormous power.

Sadly, not every situation will be easily resolved. A bully in the office, or a neighbour, or a family member, may all be difficult to deal with because they are there constantly, but I wanted to illustrate what a formidable spirit is capable of. These stories are very much in support of what I was saying in the last chapter. If we are willing to die for ourselves, there is no safer position, and no greater self-love. With that said, please try to avoid doing so! And, don't be reckless. Some people are plain dangerous, and not every challenge will end so well. Just know that the general direction of travel is an intention to find a way to stick up for yourself, and that many bullies are full of hot air when it comes to the crunch. It helps to know that.

Chapter Twenty Two - Trusting Yourself

"Having your own back" includes being able to trust yourself. Trust is earned, and trust can be lost. It's one thing to make mistakes. Mistakes are forgivable but deception and betrayal may do lasting damage. We often think of trust as a moral issue, something you "should" do because it's the right thing to do, but it goes much deeper than that. Being trustworthy is not just a good moral position for the sake of convention. Without trust, everything potentially deteriorates. The things we value the most in life cannot flourish without trust.

> **Having your own back is about coming through for yourself when it matters.**

When it matters. A lot of experts these days are peddling the "You Can Be Fantastic In Every Waking Moment" message. I see it in different forms everywhere I go, and I've noticed that it often has an almost cult-like following, which makes it next to impossible to challenge publicly. This kind of thinking makes me anxious. It's performance anxiety, and it invites us to put extreme pressure on ourselves. I don't want to be fantastic in every waking moment. I'm quite happy just being okay, and I recommend "okay" as a lifestyle if peace is your preference. Loving yourself is about figuring out what really does matter. If we don't have this clear in ourselves, we're likely to conclude that **everything** matters, and trying to do it all is not kindness, it's slavery.

Coming through for oneself does not have to involve a constant striving for perfection and brilliance. Sometimes, coming through for yourself is giving yourself permission to rest, permission to eat, permission to play, or permission to quit your job and travel the world. Being aware of your needs and desires, and taking appropriate action, is having your own back too.

The point is, we need to have a relationship with ourselves which not only says, "I've got your back" but demonstrates it too. Words are cheap. Action is meaningful. When we are consistent and reliable in listening to our needs, and delivering, we create an atmosphere of trust. You can relax in such an atmosphere. You're not unpredictable. Your inner-human knows what comes next, and that's extremely comforting.

Here's the deal. What you say to yourself matters, and what you <u>do</u> to yourself matters more.

Most of us have some bad habits. That's quite human. It would be preferable if we could not do what's not entirely good for us but many of those bad habits exist for a reason. They are coping strategies. Coming through for yourself doesn't mean living like a saint or eliminating all imperfections. It means knowing when something is truly important enough to attend to it, and then making sure that we do so. Some things just aren't that important to you. Others are. Trusting yourself involves making sure that you deliver on the things which really matter.

One approach that we definitely want to avoid, wherever possible then, is making promises to ourselves which we don't have any serious intention of keeping. This is, by definition, being a bad friend. How does it feel to be continually let down by a friend who says they'll do something and then constantly flakes out? Not good eh? So, don't do it to yourself. You don't have to promise anything if you don't want to. It's better to not make any promises than it is to repeatedly break them.

Now we seemingly have a problem though? If you want to achieve something, it's generally recognised that you'll need commitment and determination. That's a promise of sorts. How can we make a promise to ourselves and not risk breaking it?

It's really about your intention. If your friend was due to come and help you decorate, and their pet dies the night before your appointment, you're going to cut them some slack, right? This is the same. Life happens. **Your "promise" can be re-negotiated if necessary**. The rule is simple. Don't make a promise you know you probably can't or won't keep, and don't be dishonest with yourself if a reason emerges which makes your promise undeliverable. Tell the truth at all times and your relationship of trust with yourself will remain intact. That might sound like: -

"When I made this promise, I sincerely had every intention of keeping it, but the last two weeks have been simply overwhelming, and the truth is, I just

haven't got the energy to go through with it. I'm really sorry to let you down, but that's just where I am right now".

The intention was genuine. The means were unavailable.

What you definitely don't want to do, is make a promise to yourself and then pretend like you didn't. That's dishonest, and you will fall out of trust with yourself. You don't have to have an "excuse" to withdraw from an agreement. A reason is good enough. Just don't make it a regular occurrence, and remember that the degree to which you are letting yourself down relates directly to how important the promise is to you. Again, don't promise what you can't deliver.

Sometimes though, something is life and death important. Now, here's a commitment you need to make and keep. This kind of situation may have far reaching consequences for your future well-being. Even if you survive the situation, your relationship with yourself may not, if you didn't act with good intentions towards yourself.

If you're truly in dire straits, and you ask a friend to help, and they won't, it doesn't exactly secure a good relationship going forwards. Your internal relationship is the same. Your inner-human **needs** you to do something. Maybe alcohol, food, cigarettes, addiction, or self-neglect is killing you, or making life unbearable in some way? We're not talking about a few glasses of wine at the weekend here, we're talking crisis point. If this happens, we are going to need to dig deep to come through for ourselves. If you can't trust yourself in a life or death situation, then when can you trust yourself? What you say matters. What you do matters more.

There may be many obstacles to doing what needs to be done, and self-love may be the single most important factor in deciding whether the necessary action is taken or not. Sometimes, people don't have that, but it's worth understanding that self-love doesn't always begin with what you think and feel. Sometimes it starts with what you do.

A crisis is an opportunity to prove to ourselves that we care enough to do something about our emergency. We may not feel particularly loving towards ourselves, or even that we're worthy of love, but when things reach this kind of crisis point, we're going to have to dig deep and find a way to come through. That might require help from outside of ourselves. That too, is digging deep for yourself. Seek it out and don't stop until you have it. You owe yourself that.

Sometimes, even if we're at rock-bottom, this is where self-love actually begins.

The payoff, is that when you are out the other side, you've begun to re-build this essential relationship from a very deep place. If it's true that failing to deliver for yourself when you're in an emergency is a catastrophically devaluing event, then the inverse is also true. Delivering, under such circumstances, is supremely reassuring to your deepest, most vulnerable self, that you do care enough to do whatever it takes, when it matters. That's a wonderful beginning to an entirely new relationship with yourself. I know this because it's exactly what happened to me.

It's not the easiest thing in the world to know what really matters and what doesn't. It's not something anyone else can tell you either. It's very personal. One way I consider this theme though, is from the perspective of my death bed. Looking back, I ask myself whether I used my life well?

Dying people have been interviewed, and their biggest regrets include not expressing love, not resolving conflicts, not making enough time for loved ones, being defined by the expectations of others, working too much, not speaking their mind, not being true to themselves, and not recognising that happiness is a choice.

Truth is from the mouths of babes and those who are about to leave the world. These, among your personal dreams, are the matters which your deepest self wants you to deliver on, and few of them involve vanity, status, or greed. Most are about kindness, love, peace, autonomy, freedom, and fulfilment. There's no great mystery to these findings. These are the things that the human heart lives for.

Your inner-human needs to be able to trust you when it comes to sticking up for him or her on the things that matter. Attend to that, and you'll have a friend for life.

Trusting yourself is not only about how you treat yourself though. It is also about how you let other people treat you.

Culturally, we are in a difficult time right now. The term "snowflake" has been used to describe people who are too easily offended or "triggered". It describes an attitude of unrealistic entitlement to individuality and importance. The notion is one of fragility which demands to be pampered.

There was a headline a few years back about someone being sued for assault by the person whose life they saved because they'd used mouth to mouth resuscitation without permission. There's definitely a danger that we can become outraged by the merest hint of an "offence" against us, and the fair-minded among us will recognise that our obsession with our rights and personal space has just become its own worst enemy. Those who have protested about unimportant matters have undermined the voices of people who wish to air genuine grievances. Protest is now easily shut down with a single word – snowflake.

Here's what Wikipedia has to say about the term "gaslighting": -

Gaslighting is a form of psychological manipulation that seeks to sow seeds of doubt in a targeted individual or in members of a targeted group, making them question their own memory, perception, and sanity. Using persistent denial, misdirection, contradiction, and lying, it attempts to destabilize the victim and delegitimize the victim's belief.

Instances may range from the denial by an abuser that previous abusive incidents ever occurred up to the staging of bizarre events by the abuser with the intention of disorienting the victim. The term owes its origin to the 1938 Patrick Hamilton play Gaslight and its 1940 and 1944 film adaptations, in which a man dims the gas lights in his home and then persuades his wife that she is imagining the change. The term has been used in clinical and research literature, as well as in political commentary.

Both gaslighting and snowflaking seek to make you doubt yourself. They are both common tools which are used by abusers. I've explained in detail in other books how we can have a conflict between what we **want** consciously and what we **need** unconsciously. In a nutshell, you can convince yourself consciously that everything is great but your unconscious mind will produce symptoms (such as anxiety or depression) to alert you to the fact that you're not looking at something which is important and requires resolution. This is true generally, and it's true when it comes to being on the receiving end of abusive behaviour. If you've been told that you're being overly-sensitive, or being made to doubt your judgement on such matters, then you may be the victim of manipulation. If you've decided that you're okay with being treated badly, then you're manipulating yourself. It won't succeed in the long term. Conscience will always catch up with us.

Under those circumstances, it's going to be next to impossible to come into a place of true self-love because your deeper self has got the scoop on this, even if you haven't. He or she is not going to be happy about your lack of willingness to face up to the truth. You are condemning your deepest self to ongoing misery with your denial.

When you're genuinely doubting your judgement though, it's very difficult to know whether you need to make an expectation adjustment yourself, or whether the fault lies with the other person. Do you feel valued, respected, or safe? If not, then you may be on the receiving end of abuse.

It helps to have some socially agreed definitions to work with as a measure. Remember that these definitions aren't just somebody's opinion. They are drawn from years of research and data. They apply to all genders equally. The following situations are all defined as "abusive".

* Any behaviour which seeks to "control" you. Abuse by definition is about control.

* Constantly walking on eggshells around someone because they could "blow" at any moment.

* Verbal - Shouting, name-calling, blaming, undermining, shaming, or intimidation.

* Forcing or manipulating you into conforming to a particular look or standard.

* Controlling your finances.

* Preventing you from working or making your own choices about your work.

* Isolating you by stopping you from seeing friends or family and/or sabotaging those relationships.

* Laying hands on you – punching, kicking, pinching, biting, choking, slapping, pushing, spitting, poking, or any other unwanted physical actions.

* Threatening to physically harm you, someone you know, or self-harm/commit suicide unless you conform. This can include hitting walls or throwing things around. Though the threat is not direct, it is implied.

* Constant checking on your whereabouts, demanding to see proof of where you've been, or any other forms of severe mistrust. This is controlling behaviour.

* Sexual abuse – Any non-consensual sexual touch. Even if you are married or in a long-term relationship, no means no. Sex without mutual consent is considered rape in law.

* Hurt you during sex. Pressure you to do things you don't want to do. Pressure you to have unsafe sex.

* Threatening to leave/throw you out/take the children if you don't do as you are told.

* Make false allegations against you or slur your good name publicly.

* Blackmailing you with a "secret", should you speak to anyone about the abuse.

* Act jealously or possessively, or falsely accuse you of being unfaithful.

* Tell you what to think.

* Make unreasonable demands on your time or attention.

* Blame you for the abuse.

* Deny that there is abuse and make you doubt yourself.

This is a long list I know, but I included it here because every single one of these points needs spelling out. Some people think that being on the receiving end of these behaviours is quite normal. It isn't. This is by no means an exhaustive list. Bullying, harassment, and abuse, can come in a variety of forms from any person in any place. In the list above, we may see some definitions which don't automatically require that we label ourselves as victims of abuse. Take shouting for instance. It happens sometimes. In my 25+ years of mostly happy marriage, there have been a few shouting matches with no harm done. I certainly wouldn't call myself a victim or survivor of abuse, and neither would Mrs C. Obviously, we need to use common sense when interpreting this list. It's included here though to highlight that we can be rather too accepting of abusive behaviour on occasion because we believe it's "normal". This just helps us to get a handle on the fact, that often, it's not.

If any of these events happen just once, then it may be as simple as explaining to the person you are in relationship with, that they crossed a line. The next chapter will explain how to do that. Generally, the advice though, is that if you experience any of these boundary breaching behaviours **repeatedly**, particularly if you've made your position clear that it's not okay with you, then you **must** recognise that your relationship is toxic, and get out. Research shows clearly that people who abuse, even once, generally go on to repeat abuse. Once is a warning. Twice is practically a guarantee. Don't kid yourself that it will stop. The longer you remain in a toxic relationship, the more drained you will become. Get out while you still have strength. Don't even hesitate. There's nothing to second guess. It's a crystal-clear decision. Stay and continue to be abused, or leave and get well. Don't let any "I'm sorry, it will never happen again" or "I'm too weak for you to leave me." stuff get in the way. Yes, we know they're really nice to you most of the time. It doesn't matter. Abuse is abuse. It should not be tolerated, and it will happen again. If you don't believe me, then head on over to one of the following resources to hear it from someone else.

There are many excellent and caring resources, out there online, from cyber-bullying to workplace bullying, to domestic violence to "should I break up with my friend" sites. Many of these sites are country specific, so I'll leave it with you to web search them, as the resources offered will often be local. If you're in a controlling relationship, remember to cover your tracks by deleting your browsing history if you visit abuse support sites. Such a partner will likely not respond well to knowing that you've taken the step of informing yourself.

Two trustworthy sites that I will mention though, are:-

Helpguide.org which is linked to Harvard University https://www.helpguide.org/home-pages/abuse.htm containing the best resource links for US readers.

For the UK I recommend the charity Mind as a good starting point:- https://www.mind.org.uk/information-support/guides-to-support-and-services/abuse/#.XAT_Fmj7RPY

Your inner human is potentially the best friend you have in the world. If you see your best friend in an abusive relationship, you don't stand by silently and watch them be destroyed, do you? Well, your inner human deserves every bit as much care as your best friend. Make him or her an absolute priority. When your self is in peril, coming through when it matters is the highest form of self-love. Don't fear the snowflake label. Sticks and stones may break your bones and abusers do really hurt you. There's nothing snowflake about that. Get help if you need it. It's out there.

This is every bit as important in building trust with yourself as the way you treat yourself directly.

Not every indiscretion towards us is abuse. There's the rough and tumble of everyday living where people are rushed, rude, abrupt, absent-minded, or selfish. Going to pieces over minor indiscretions is likely to be unnecessary. Instead, we just need to speak up…and speak up clearly.

Chapter Twenty Three – Owning Your Voice

I want to share an amusing tale with you. Earlier this year, Mrs C and I went to Spain for a week. On the outward journey, our flight was delayed for over six hours. We arrived at our hotel, late and exhausted, after a three am start. We had a few celebratory drinks and went to bed. The next day, the combination of exhaustion, slight hangover, and morning hunger, made for a shaky start to the day. We walked around the corner to a very busy patisserie to grab a tea and croissant to start the day. We've been in this shop before. It's always hectic. The counter staff are famously impatient, so we knew what to expect. My Spanish skills are basic. We were browsing the display. The lady at the counter was shouting at us in Spanish. We said "one minute please". She huffed and puffed, and a horde of people came rushing in through the front door. This made her shout at us more loudly. We didn't understand a word, but she was basically screaming "Come on! Hurry up! What do you want?" I tried my best Spanish and she just shouted some more.

In a panic then, Mrs C pushed me to get out of the way. The new horde of people swarmed all around us, and I tried to push my way through them (no orderly queuing here!) to get out. I made it a couple of steps before I was stopped dead by somebody standing on my shoelace. I turned to make an evasive move, and as I did so, I managed to swipe a young boy who was sat in a chair eating his croissant, with my backpack. The lady was still shouting at us. The horde was swarming. Mrs C was pushing me from behind, telling me to move, admonishing me for hitting the kid with my pack, and I was stuck fast! It was a moment of complete comic chaos. Somehow, we made it outside, laughing, but we were genuinely stressed out. Neither of us were willing to go back in that day. We found somewhere else to get breakfast.

We were both surprisingly shaken though, which on the face of it seems utterly ridiculous. It was hardly life-threatening but it was mildly humiliating. As we searched for another café we discussed that we now felt quite anxious, and this was particularly notable because Mrs C doesn't usually feel anxious about very much at all. It was there, that this chapter was conceived. I pondered on why such a minor infraction had caused us to feel quite so disturbed. Apart from the fact that we were a little shaky anyway, it was, I realised, primarily because we didn't have a voice when we needed it.

It's not the first time I've experienced this. I often feel quite vulnerable in non-English speaking countries. My French is pretty good. My Spanish is okay, but elsewhere my vocabulary extends to about thirty words. I'm a lover, not a fighter. I use my clarity and my voice to get myself out of a tight spot. When I don't have one, I am acutely aware that I am at an extreme disadvantage. I cannot make my feelings or my intentions known, and I have no way to defend myself.

Maybe you can relate to this? It highlights to me just how **vital** it is that we can speak up for ourselves when we need to. A lack of language skills though is not the only reason that we may find ourselves silenced. If we do not think that we are "good enough" to have a voice worth listening to, or that we are so emotionally confused or stressed that we can't articulate our case, then we may find ourselves in an extremely vulnerable position.

Having a voice in life is central to our well-being, but many people fear sharing their voice in case it is judged harshly, or because they don't recognize that they have a right to speak up for themselves. We Brits can be particularly understated at times, and we're rarely quite sure where the line is between confidence and arrogance. The best way to know the difference is to remember that confidence is a rising tide which lifts all boats, and arrogance thinks it's an island. Keep that in mind and you won't go too far wrong.

"Be yourself – everyone else is taken." – Oscar Wilde

Authenticity is a daring act of courage at the best of times. Being authentic, means being yourself even if there are elements of your personality which other people may think poorly of. It also includes embracing elements of your personality which **you** may think poorly of. Now, that's challenging, right? I mean, if you think something about you is flawed, it sounds like insanity to bring it out and wear it in full view for everyone else to see (and judge). Why would we do that?

Let me share with you another personal story. I left school at the age of sixteen with some fairly pitiful examination results. It was not an uncommon occurrence for more than one member of my family to deliver an insult veiled as a joke whenever I displayed some intelligence. That side of my family line were largely skilled manual workers, and they were good at what they did, but there was a reverse snobbery in my family line. "Intellectuals" represented a different class of people, and they were considered "not to be trusted." Unconsciously, they didn't want me to become that. A similar attitude existed in my school too, with many children being from similar family backgrounds. Looking back, I can see that I dumbed myself down to fit in. The result was that I left school having fulfilled little of my potential, and I spent the next twenty years in relative poverty, furiously scrambling to build something out of nothing.

What would have happened if I'd had a voice?

Perhaps I would have said…

"I've noticed that when I share my academic successes or aspirations with you, the response I receive is rarely encouraging, and sometimes it seems to me that you actually disapprove. I feel really hurt when you put me down for showing that I'm capable because it feels like you're asking me to choose between being loved by you, or fulfilling my potential. I'm obviously going to opt for the being loved option because being unloved feels pretty awful. I really don't want to be asked to make that choice. What I'd really like from you is some encouragement and validation for doing well at school, and that you'll still love me. Can you give me that?"

How much difference might that conversation have made to the next twenty years of my life? Though not certain, it's entirely possible that the "shame" that they "dumped" on me for displaying intelligence would have been handed right back to them. It's likely that I would have seen an attitude adjustment overnight, and maybe received a little encouragement rather than scorn.

Alas, I was too young and powerless to understand such things. My inner-intellectual was expertly hidden for many years, and he was not recovered until relatively recently.

You see, I took **their** beliefs on board. Not only was I encouraged to hide my own intelligence, I was also encouraged to judge and berate others for daring to display theirs. In our school, as in many of that era, if you were a high academic achiever you received the label of "boffin", and it wasn't intended as a compliment. Boffins got bullied. You didn't want to be a boffin. The attitude of certain members of my family were undoubtedly absorbed from a similar environment. None of us stood a chance really, from our families, or the school cultures.

The consequences of failing to speak up for myself, was twenty years of terrible jobs and fairly constant financial insecurity. Even in my early adult life, I did not understand how to do so. Authenticity is not easy. We need to have enough love for ourselves to be willing to speak up, speak out, and then self-protect when the inevitable fallout comes. That means doing the right thing, even though it's not necessarily the easy thing.

There is a measure of inevitability about unkindness in the schoolyard, and we're unlikely to have the skills necessary to self-protect when we're twelve years old but bullying or controlling behaviour can, and does, continue into later life. Now we have a jealous friend, a bitter colleague, a sadistic boss, or an abusive partner. They all have an agenda to disrespect or undermine us in some way. The number one tool we have at our disposal here is our voice, so let's use it!

In many ways, this book has been leading up to this moment. What I hope to have instilled in you, is the clearest understanding that you have a right to have a voice. When you love yourself, you speak from a clear heart, unbound by hate, fear, doubt, or insignificance. You matter. You have value, and if you have something to say, then say it. Nobody is forced to listen. Those who don't want to hear you, can move along. No harm done. You have every right to protect your hard-earned peace.

In my book, *Anxiety Relief*, I covered "boundaries and assertiveness" in full detail. As a writer, I'm keen to avoid repetition but I also recognise that not everyone will have read that book, so I'm going to just briefly skim some key points here.

* Boundaries are limits. Boundaries refer to what is, or what is not, okay with you. Personal boundaries are the limits you set for your own protection. They could relate to absolutely anything, but you can think of them as protection for your time, attention, personal space, your values, your goals, and your beliefs. For example, you can have boundaries around how much time, attention, or money someone is demanding from you. Or, you might want to set limits on how often you think it's okay for somebody to keep telling you that you're wrong about something. You are the person who knows yourself best. Your boundaries should never be dictated to you by someone else. Everybody has a right to have boundaries. In owning your own boundaries, you must also recognise the right of others to own theirs. It's a two-way street.

* Assertiveness is communicating where your limits are, to others, and specifically letting them know if they breach them, either intentionally, or unintentionally. It is possible to be **gracefully assertive**. Assertiveness is not an act of aggression. It is simply letting others know where the line is, and saying that it's not okay with **you** when that line is crossed. It is not about them. It is about you. Assertiveness is letting others know what your needs and wishes are and requesting that they respect them.

* We all have an internal rulebook. Your rulebook contains rules such as: - It's not okay to kill, steal, harm, intimidate, abuse, deceive, miss appointments, be late, shout at customers, undermine my friends etc. You cannot assume that other people have the exact same rules in their internal rulebook as you have in yours. What seems obvious to you about how people should treat each other, may not be obvious to the person you are dealing with. On a first offence then, it is your job to let the other person know that you have a rule which you would like them to be aware of, and respect, going forwards.

Nobody can insult you without your permission. Remember that silence in the face of poor treatment amounts to permission. You have a right to remove that permission.

* We communicate our rules to others using a non-aggressive four step format, which is as follows: -

a) State what happened. Stick to the facts. "When "X" happened"...

b) Explain how it made you feel. Do not use accusatory language. Just say how it made you feel. "It made me feel "X"...

c) Now explain why it made you feel that way, "Because"...

d) Finally, ask the person to help you in settling the issue. You may need to be specific (i.e I don't ever want to hear you make jokes about my nose again).

Now, let's return briefly to the hypothetical statement I made earlier when I was referring to the teasing I received around displaying intelligence in my formative years:-

"(a) I've noticed that when I share my academic successes or aspirations with you that the response I receive is rarely encouraging, and sometimes it seems to me that you actually disapprove. (b) I feel really hurt when you put me down for showing that I'm capable (c) because it feels like you're asking me to choose between being loved by you or fulfilling my potential. I'm obviously going to opt for the being loved option because being unloved feels pretty awful. I really don't want to be asked to make that choice. (d) What I'd really like from you is some encouragement and validation for doing well at school, and that you'll still love me. Can you give me that?"

If you analyse that statement you will notice that it is delivered in the a,b,c,d format explained above. There is a statement of fact, an explanation of how it makes me feel, why it makes me feel that way, and a request for things to change. It doesn't attack anyone. It's not manipulative. It's a clear statement explaining my position, nothing more. The response we receive to such messages should tell us everything we need to know about how the other person intends to treat us, going forwards. If they say, "I hear you. I respect you. I care how you feel. I have no wish to harm you. I will do my best to treat you in the way that you wish to be treated", then you have a healthy situation. Any other response, whether that be anger, argument, ignorance, feigned interest, excuses, or a flat "no" without explanation, is really code for, "I have no intention to treat you well". Further discussion is perfectly reasonable. Disinterest, denial of your right to have those feelings, or an unwillingness to engage on the matter, is not. Remaining in relationship with someone who has no intention of treating you well is a form of self-abuse.

As far as relationships are concerned then, I have one piece of straight to the point advice for you, which comes in two parts.

One: - If a person you are in relationship with is treating you in a way which makes you feel devalued, disrespected, dumped upon, taken from, used, abused, unsupported, unloved, unappreciated, or any other type of awful, then silence on your part amounts to agreement, and permission for them to carry on treating you that way.

Remember these words: -

> **Love doesn't hurt. If being in this relationship hurts more than it soothes, <u>it's not love.</u>**

It is your job to let that person know how you feel and be specific about what they are doing which is causing you to experience that feeling around them. Then listen. They may have a valid explanation. If they do have an explanation, then talk it through with them to arrive at a position where everyone's circumstances and needs are honoured.

If they don't, you need to tell them in clear terms that the current dynamic is not okay with you and explain how you would like it to change. Be willing to hear their side of the story and agree to make changes yourself if fair and necessary. If their demands don't seem fair to you, tell them why, and keep talking until you reach agreement. If you can't reach agreement, then I'm afraid that relationship is probably over.

Two: - If they are hostile to your communication (unwilling to communicate), unwilling to change their behaviour towards you, or continually disregard your new agreements, then there is only one course of action which can be called an act of self-love. That is to leave that relationship. Remaining in a relationship with someone who repeatedly abuses you in some way is self-abuse by proxy, and a sure way to erode any trust you have developed with yourself. That's not standing up for yourself, and your inner-human will not be pleased. Anxiety or depression could follow.

This, in itself, is crucial to your happiness in life, but there is another less obvious reason to know how and why to do this. Being willing to walk away, if necessary, puts you in a position of great safety in your relationships. This is not something to be used as a whip or an ultimatum. This is about self-protection, not attack. Throwing "I'll leave" around as a threat is emotional blackmail, and it's likely to backfire spectacularly. When a willingness to walk away is held with power, it should probably not be spoken during negotiations. It is something which is held in the heart as an absolute last resort, and may only be spoken when all other attempts at reconciliation have failed. Then, it is not a bargaining chip. It has become a simple fact, and it should be one you are willing to implement.

Assuming that your intention is to treat your relationships with respect and value, then valuing yourself enough to know that you'll walk away from anyone who repeatedly treats you poorly means that you need not live in fear of being let down, cheated on, betrayed, abused, or unloved.

Your position switches from a fear of being abandoned, to recognising that if they screw it up, they lose you. Not the other way around. You hold the cards, not them.

If somebody continually fails to uphold their end of the relationship, then it is for you to know that you have been a good and loyal friend. If they wreck the relationship, that is on them, not you. You have not been a bad person in ending that relationship. They have not given you a choice. If you cannot be in relationship with that person and not be in a situation where you are agreeing to be treated poorly by them, then your priority must be to yourself. Ultimately, when you love yourself enough, you will recognise that the real loss is theirs.

Walking away from any relationship is painful, costly, and not a decision to be taken lightly. In addition, it could potentially involve turning your life upside down. People who love each other will fall out from time to time. Love involves working through that, wherever possible. Neither can we expect one hundred percent from some people, all the time. Your parents might drive you crazy, half the time, but that's a huge one to walk away from. Your friend might be disorganised generally. You don't need to take it personally. Your partner says some horrible things. It's out of character. You discover that they are under enormous pressure elsewhere. These are not reasons to assume you're being mistreated. There is such a thing as making allowances for people. The key word here is **repeatedly.** If you've asked someone to change their behaviour towards you, and they don't show any signs of honouring your needs or wishes, then that's how you'll know it's not you. It's them.

If they are wounded, it's **their** responsibility to get help, not your duty to try to heal them, so don't let them make excuses for their behaviour. A failure to address their emotional issues is an abdication of responsibility on their part, and it's not your job to continually be on the receiving end of that. It actually gives them permission to do nothing while you pick up the bill.

I must acknowledge that there are some situations which are extremely tricky to navigate, a difficult boss or colleague at work, for instance. You need to pay the rent or mortgage. You can't afford to walk out, or risk being fired. A violent neighbour who you can't get away from is equally difficult to escape. If it's your marriage which is in trouble, you have to consider the children. These are life's tough spots. In theory, you **should** be able to be assertive in any situation, including a workplace, but it's not always the wise move, and with some people you'll be wasting your breath. Not all humans are reasonable. It's therefore worth saying that sometimes things are better left unsaid. If you know that the truth may lead to shooting yourself in the foot, or crushing someone's feelings unnecessarily, maybe it's kinder and wiser to hold back on your right to be assertive. You'll need to use your better judgement as to when to hold your tongue, but if you're in an intolerable situation, just make sure that you start planning your exit strategy as soon as possible, and follow through on it. Living under those circumstances with no end in sight is a recipe for depression and anxiety.

Knowing in your heart that you'd be willing to walk away from any relationship which is damaging to you is a valuable protection to have in place. If you're skilful enough, and surround yourself with the right people, you may never need to use it. You still need to have it to hand though if you want to feel truly safe in your own skin.

As a final point on this matter, one of the great bonuses you can receive from learning how to embrace and express your authenticity, is that you'll also learn to honour others who do the same. Instead of feeling threatened or "told off" when somebody asks you to treat them in a certain way, you'll find that you have a frame of reference for why they are doing so in your own rulebook. The new rule is "people have a right to let others know how they wish to be treated".

A person with low self-worth on the receiving end of a boundary assertion will usually interpret the word "no", or any other assertive communication, as a rejection of who they are, rather than a communication relating to the request itself. There's an unconscious assumption that they received a negative response because they are not valuable enough to receive help. A person with a strong sense of self-worth will interpret the word "no" as being about the wishes and needs of the other. They will probably have said no to whoever asked. In short, it's not personal. With a strong sense of self-worth in place, asking for what you want, then becomes much less frightening because a no is not going to be crushing. We simply accept that the response was about the other person's needs. We choose not to judge them or ourselves because of it, and we move on.

Chapter Twenty Four – Anxiety And Your Mind

This book wouldn't be complete without considering the role that your everyday thoughts play in how you feel about yourself. Up to this point, the spotlight has been on matters of the heart, but our brains can generate a lot of mental noise when we are stressed out generally.

Here's the formula: -

Negativity creates stress. Stress converts to anxiety. Anxiety must find a focus.

In practice, this means that when our stress levels are elevated, our brains tend to become more obsessive and hyper-vigilant. The brain will then go searching for a "reason" that we are feeling so anxious. Human brains aren't particularly accurate in this regard. They have a habit of seizing upon the first thing which presents as a potential threat, and often these themes are highly irrational. This then becomes the focus of the anxiety. If the thing that scares you the most in the world is the fear that you might be an awful person in some way, then that will be the thing that your anxious mind will fixate upon.

In truth, the anxiety we feel is usually **not** about that one thing. Our stresses are caused by multiple areas in our lives, but our minds don't always recognise these factors, and all of our stress gets pinned on one or two central obsessions. This might manifest as "I'm too fat" or "My nose is too big", or "Everybody hates me", or "Maybe I'm dangerous to be around". These thoughts can then loop round and round in the mind, and consume us, making us more and more anxious each day.

At the extreme end of this, we can see such concerns as "What if it turns out that I'm a paedophile?", or, "What if I lose control and stab somebody with a knife?" These extreme irrational thoughts can cause perfectly good-hearted people to avoid being around children or remove all the knives from their home, in the mistaken belief that they might "accidentally" act out their worries. When thoughts are this extreme, it's usually part of a serious anxiety disorder called obsessive compulsive disorder (OCD). This condition is a liar, plain and simple. Don't believe a word of it.

When such disturbances occur, the very first thing we need to establish, is that the brain is essentially malfunctioning and sending us erroneous signals. The feelings will seem very real and extremely alarming but we must not make the mistake of "buying into" those irrational thoughts as if they were true. The moment we start believing those thoughts are true is the moment that we start to get into truly scary territory.

The correct position, is to recognise that those scary thoughts are nothing more than a worried, misfiring brain, trying to find something to pin the worry on. We actually know better than it does what is truly a threat, and what isn't, and we have to keep gently reminding our poor overheated brain that everything is **just fine**! In addition, we must not **act** as if those concerns were real. This is not easy, but it is the correct procedure if we want to halt the process.

Please take careful note of what I'm about to tell you then.

It is possible for somebody to have a perfectly healthy relationship with themselves, but still feel awful about themselves, when they are very stressed out.

I consider myself to be a person who has a fundamentally great relationship with myself. Make no mistake about it though, when my stress levels are elevated, my self-confidence will take a hit. Anxiety and stress are extremely de-stabilising. When this happens, we need to remember that it is a **symptom** of stress overload, and not an indication that we have fallen out of friendship with ourselves. In other words, it's temporary. When our stress levels reduce again, we will find that everything is all fine and good, exactly as we left it. This is an additional reason that it's important to have a good relationship with yourself. In times of stress, we want to be able to remember that we are good people, and support ourselves. If we don't like ourselves anyway, it's going to be a rougher ride because those feelings of worthlessness will be more difficult to refute.

If you have not been able to make this book work for you, it may be because your stress levels are too high. That's not a get-out clause on my part. It's a genuine pointer to what might be getting in the way of you improving your well-being. My book, Anxiety Relief, can help you in this regard.

In any case, it's important to know that our sense of self-worth/esteem/confidence is likely to suffer when we are overly-stressed generally, and we should factor that in before we decide that we have a whole bunch of "issues" which need dealing with. If you recognise that you felt fine with yourself before your recent stresses came along, and now you feel awful about yourself for no good reason, there's every chance that your problem is not you, but your stress levels. That will require that you look at the other areas of your life where stress is being generated and take positive action there. Meanwhile, we want to see the internal disharmony as just an inevitable symptom of stress, and know that it will pass when calm returns.

If we are unlucky enough to find ourselves in one of these stress-loops, we'll need to take the reins for a while because temporarily our brains aren't doing what they are supposed to. When we're calm, the brain is focussed on what's good in life. When we're anxious, the brain can generate all kind of worries to alarm us. Our job then, is to continually correct these irrational thoughts until things get back to normal again.

Here then, are a few pointers drawn from Cognitive Behavioural Therapy (CBT) to help you challenge those scary thoughts when they arise.

* Sometimes your thoughts will make you believe that your self-worth is dependent on some other condition being fulfilled. We want to remember that our self-worth is **always** valid. Such a thought might be something like, "I MUST pass this test, or else I'll be a complete failure."

Identify the thoughts where you are using "imperative" language such as "must, ought to, should, have to, or need to". This language suggests that if you don't fulfil the condition, then the result will say something catastrophic about you. That's a huge amount of pressure which places you in a win/lose scenario. Remember what we said earlier about everything being an experiment?

Replace imperative language with softer words like "I'd like to, it would be really nice if, or I'd prefer". Then the statement becomes "*It would be really nice* if I pass this test first time around but my best is good enough, and if I don't nail it this time, I'll re-take it. I'm proud of myself for giving it a go, whatever happens."

* If your mind is producing thoughts which tell you that you're an awful person in some way, then sit down with a pen and paper, draw a line down the middle of the paper splitting it into columns. Title the left-hand column "Evidence that this thought is true" and the right-hand column with "Evidence against this thought".

Complete each column with as many "facts" as you can think of. Include nice things you do for yourself, help you provide to others, your work-related accomplishments, the people who love you, ways in which you put others first, your talents and humour. Unless you really are a monster (I doubt that!), you should find that your evidence shows quite clearly that while you may not get everything right all the time, on balance, you are a very kind and worthy person most of the time. Condense the essence of that message into a sentence or two and stick it on your fridge!

* Come up with a list of at least thirty positive traits which apply to you, some, if not all of the time. See if you can connect an example of a time when you've displayed that trait in your own mind. Maybe close your eyes and remember some sweet times for a while...

* Again, using a pen and paper, write a letter to your deepest self. Speak from the heart. Tell him that you understand the difficulties he has faced in life. Tell him that you're sorry that he has had to endure real pain at times. Don't dwell too much on the pain but just acknowledge it deeply. Then tell him why he's awesome! Explain to him that you are committed to his well-being from this point forwards, and ask his forgiveness for any screw-ups so far. Give him a realistic but heartfelt pep-talk. Sell him a future you both can be proud of. Don't forget...don't promise what you can't or won't deliver. If you have "hopes", then call them that, not

promises. It's your letter. Say whatever else you think he needs to hear from you. Keep this letter handy and refer to it whenever you need it. It will remind you of what you (truly) believe and feel in your deepest self, which should look a lot different from the nonsense an anxious brain might throw at you.

* Finally, be mindful of the language you use when speaking to yourself or conversing with others. If you're someone who says "sorry" for every tiny thing, stop doing that! Sorry is reserved for genuine apologies only. If you constantly apologise over nothing, you're sending a message back to yourself that you have to apologise for being. You don't. None of us do. The same goes for any other communication which says "Please don't notice me. I'm not good enough to be here". We're here. Everyone else will have to get used to it.

If you hear yourself saying nasty things to yourself like "I'll never be any good", stop doing that too. I won't labour the point. Just don't, okay?

Chapter Twenty Five - You've Got This!

I'm usually the first to remind people to be aware of their **limitations,** as well as their greatness, and I'm painfully aware that those well-intended pep-talks which encourage you to be the very best version of yourself aren't always helpful. For those who aren't in a position to implement such advice, the likely outcome is a feeling of failure. I don't want that for you.

This book will have provided different things for different people. Perhaps for some, deep healing. For others, food for thought. It's not a race, and it's not a competition. Sometimes words plant seeds which may ultimately germinate many years later. There is a lot to digest here. I know that.

I hope, however, that I've managed, at the very least, to successfully transmit a "feeling", or atmosphere, to you, which connects you with something you may have felt stirring within yourself but unable to define or articulate. Your inner human and my inner human are ultimately made of the same stuff. We share our Humanity. It is common to us. No matter what your personal story is, your original innocence exists within you as surely as it is within all of us. It awaits your attention and your friendship. If I've helped you to remember this about yourself, then I've accomplished the minimum requirements of my mission.

Beyond that, I hope also to have furnished you with information and tools which have helped, or will help you to take your relationship with yourself to a new level, ideally all the way to being best friends forever. And, if you already had the basics in place when you picked this book up, I hope to have confirmed, validated, and strengthened what you already knew.

As the author, I want to remind you that for all my so-called expertise on these matters, I can have my moments of weakness. I don't always say no when I should. I don't always speak up for myself because I can't be bothered with the discomfort that doing so inevitably entails. I do let my friends and family get away with behaviours which aren't entirely healthy. I do let myself down from time to time too. I don't see these as failings though. Attempting to have a perfect record on self-love and emotional protection is just another stick we can beat ourselves with.

True self-love includes recognizing that we're going to screw self-love itself up on occasion. Then we go back to accepting what is, saying sorry if it's warranted, and re-connecting deeply with that beautiful innocent presence within ourselves who invariably finds this hard-knock world pretty darned challenging at the best of times.

I have a particular fondness for the word "cherish". For me, purely personally, the sound of the word conjures up an association with the love-blood-red of cherries, and the angelic lightness of cherubs. It feels like a huge, warm, safe, cuddle which says, "Everything is alright Sweetheart. You are safe. You are forgiven. You are loved". To know that I am cherished feels like more than just being loved. It feels like I am the most precious thing in the world to someone. I want my inner human to know that that's how I feel about him. Okay, I know that sounds gushy, but it's private (or, at least, it was!) Sometimes I look at the people I love in the world and I feel the same way. If I told them, they'd probably retch! We're not going to swoon around all day on a cloud of self-congratulations. This is the stuff you're going to use when you need that cuddle!

I'm going to finish, predictably, with the same message that every one of my books has carried. The world needs healing. Healing the world begins with healing yourself. It's hard work, healing, but for whatever reason, it seems that when you get a human body, you also get a broken heart at some point. Broken hearts turn sour if they're not attended to, and sour hearts ruin lives.

The pain of not healing far outweighs the pain of facing our demons. Healing and demons are not mutually exclusive. They, like failure and success, are actually part of the same continuum. The fiercer our demons are, the stronger our love will become. Only an equal force will do it.

Our demons must ultimately be loved into transformation. Our demons cannot be destroyed. They can only be transformed. They do not go easily however.

There is only one force in this existence which has the power to transform those demons, and that is Love. And, there is only one person in existence with the power to wield that love with the sincerity required to heal **your** broken heart, and that is **you**. Kindness is the expression of that. Dig deep my friends…and be good to yourselves and each other…

…You've got this!

One Last Thing

I hope you have enjoyed this book! Thank you for reading. If it has helped you, please be kind enough to leave a review on the Amazon book page. Just a few moments of your time will mean more to me than you'd think, and may help other readers who need these words, to find them.

Thank you enormously!

To leave a review on Amazon UK -
www.amazon.co.uk/dp/B07M6Z778N

To leave a review on Amazon USA -
www.amazon.com/dp/B07M6Z778N

Stay Connected

I'd love to stay connected with you. Please do join me by signing up for my readers group at: - www.youcanfixyouranxiety.com/stay-connected

You'll receive two free super soothing, life affirming hypnotherapeutic recordings to use and keep and I'll keep you updated with news of new releases with special offers for reader's group subscribers. No spam guaranteed and you can unsubscribe at any time.

Or come over and join me by liking my Facebook page at: -
https://www.facebook.com/johncrawfordauthor

How To Love Your Inner Human is available in ebook and paperback format from Amazon, and audio book from Audible. You can get the audio book absolutely free of charge when you make it your first audio book with Audible's 30 day free trial. You must cancel within 30 days to avoid charges (or stay with Audible if you like it), but either way, you keep the audio book forever. Check out a sample below.

https://www.youcanfixyouranxiety.com/inner-human-audio

Other Works By This Author

"Anxiety Relief" is a full 312 pages (paperback), and covers just about everything you need to know about stress and anxiety, and how to resolve it. An Amazon UK bestseller since September 2017, this is a book which truly delivers on its promise.

You can find this book at these links: -

Amazon UK - www.amazon.co.uk/dp/B01EAZN8HM

Amazon USA - www.amazon.com/dp/B077X2NWFJ

(The USA version has a different paperback cover)

You can also go the website at www.youcanfixyouranxiety.com if you'd like to learn more about the books.

Using fictional case studies from real world examples, *Anger Management* will explore clearly why you may feel so much anger in your being, and explain why your subconscious programming is making it impossible for you to "will" yourself calm. With that understood you'll find practical, workable approaches here, to understand and desensitise your triggers, live more peacefully, enjoy better relationship security, be more patient with the world, and get more of what you need without the stress or regret of anger and rage.

You can find this book at these links: -

Amazon UK - www.amazon.co.uk/dp/B01HENG6LW

Amazon USA - www.amazon.com/dp/B01HENG6LW

Are you grounded by fear? Convinced of catastrophe? Longing for the exotic? *Onwards And Upwards* is a unique five step program designed to have you flying with confidence in less than two hours.

Onwards And Upwards also comes loaded with two specially recorded professional hypnotherapy sessions which can be downloaded and used both before and during your travels.

Written with a lightness of spirit and exuding care for your well-being throughout, you'll find this easy and illuminating read a joy.

Are you ready to reclaim your wings? Let *Onwards And Upwards* show you how it's done!

Amazon UK - www.amazon.co.uk/dp/B079P4BGMF

Amazon USA - www.amazon.com/dp/B079P4BGMF

Free Book Offer

And...just a reminder in case you didn't grab it at the beginning.

As a valued reader, I'd like to invite you to join me by becoming a member of my free reader's group and download my third book "Dear Anxiety: This Is My Life" PLUS two professionally recorded relaxation recordings delivering authentic hypnosis experiences for beating stress. – All **absolutely free of charge.** No strings. Just sign up with your email address. I'll add you to the group and keep you updated with news and offers. You can unsubscribe at any time. Here's the link:-

www.youcanfixyouranxiety.com/amazon-book-free-gift

About John Crawford

John Crawford is truly qualified to share expertise on how to overcome anger, anxiety, OCD, and depression. Not only has he been a professional therapist for more than fourteen years, he was himself held hostage by severe anxiety and depression for many years in his twenties. His understanding of the field is therefore more than purely intellectual. It's deeply personal and committed.

John ran his own thriving business as a one to one hypnotherapist/psychotherapist specialising in the treatment of anxiety, depression, and OCD, from 2003-2016. He quickly gained a solid professional reputation in the Bristol and Bath area of the UK for anxiety-related difficulties. He has over seven thousand hours of clinical experience in helping people to overcome their emotional and mental health challenges.

After a year off to launch his writing career in 2016, he returned to work as a therapist in 2017-18 and finally became a full-time author in June 2018. He is no longer offering one to one therapeutic services, as writing is now his sole focus.

He is a significant contributor of sections of the training materials used by Clifton Practice Hypnotherapy Training (CPHT), a now international Hypnotherapy Training Centre with twelve branches in the United Kingdom. CPHT is recognised for its outstanding Solution-Focussed Brief Therapy training.

John has spoken professionally for the Association for Professional Hypnosis and Psychotherapy, Clifton Practice Hypnotherapy Training, OCD Action (the largest national OCD charity in the UK), as well as regularly at smaller supervisory events for local practitioners. He has also written for the highly respected online anxiety sufferers' resource, No More Panic.

He was a registered and accredited member of three leading therapeutic organisations - Association for Professional Hypnosis & Psychotherapy, National Hypnotherapy Society, and National Council of Psychotherapists, up until 2016 when he closed his one to one practice to focus on writing and teaching. His main qualifications include:-

Diploma in Hypnotherapy and Psychotherapy - Clifton Practice Training (formerly EICH)

Hypnotherapy Practitioner Diploma - National externally (NCFE) accredited to NVQ 4.

Diploma in Cognitive Behavioural Hypnotherapy - Externally (NCFE) accredited to NVQ4.

Anxiety Disorders Specialist Certification - The Minnesota Institute of Advanced Communication Skills.

He lives happily in Bristol (UK) with his wife and cat.

Full Copyright Notice

How To Love Your Inner Human In A World Of Anxiety

Self Help Solutions To Not Feeling Good Enough

By

JOHN CRAWFORD

ISBN-10: 1794226486

ISBN-13: 978-1794226487

Copyright © 2019 by John Crawford

All rights reserved. First Published: February 2019

www.youcanfixyouranxiety.com

No part of this book may be reproduced in any form or by any electronic or mechanical means including information storage and retrieval systems, without permission in writing from the author. Short quotes are permissible providing that credit is given to this author in the quoting work.

Every effort has been made in the writing of this book to give credit where it is due, including short quotes, and there is no intention to infringe upon any copyrights. If you believe that there is any part of this work which infringes your intellectual property in any way please let me know and I will gladly remove it immediately.

Please visit: http://www.youcanfixyouranxiety.com for updates, offers, news, enquiries, and events.

Printed in Great Britain
by Amazon